MW00816827

FEAR NOT

365 DAYS A YEAR

A Devotional For Courage

Sandra Darlene Davis

FEAR NOT
365 DAYS A YEAR

A Devotional For Courage

Editor Christy Smith

Sandra Darlene Davis

All Scripture taken from the English Standard Version of the Bible. (ESV) unless noted otherwise by verse.

Whosoever Press books may be ordered through booksellers or by contacting:

Whosoever Press
10749 AL Hwy 168
Boaz, AL 35957

www.WhosoeverPress.com

1-256-706-3315

ISBN-13: 978-0998772493

Library of Congress Control Number: Applied For

Printed in the United States of America

Whosoever Press Date: 1/1/2018

Dedication

This journal about courage is dedicated to Michael Dwinnon Helms, known to his friends as Mike. Mike was my life partner, my soulmate, and my helper. Mike died on July 1, 2017, after fighting a terrible battle with a tree and a brain tumor.

On April 20, 2017, he had a car accident. He had head injuries as well as six broken bones. After being airlifted to University of Alabama Trauma Center, the doctors discovered that Mike had a large, aggressive brain tumor. They told the family as well as Mike about the tumor in the emergency room.

After two surgeries, and 15 days in the hospital, Mike had to go to rehabilitation. He struggled with pain from broken bones, left side paralysis, and brain injury as well as the tumor. As his body healed, his brain tumor got worse. He tried to get well for almost two months before the battle ended. He fought all the way. He was a true warrior. He never gave up. He never asked for the battle to end.

As long as he was able to speak, he was polite to everyone. He would tell the staff how much he appreciated the care. I believe he came to know the

Lord more intimately. Then, at the facility, for the first time in twenty years, he asked to go to church, and we attended church service together, even though he had to be wheeled in.

Every day, starting two days before the accident, I read the daily verse from this devotional to Mike. It seemed to offer him comfort. It was a great comfort to me. I was amazed at how one year after writing these words; they had tremendous power to heal me. It was uncanny the way some verses pertained to the trial we were facing that day.

Mike, you patiently watched me work on this manuscript for one year. Then together we lived the journey and faced our worst nightmare with strength and bravery. You taught me to be strong. I will always love you.

Table Of Contents

INTRODUCTION

Jesus Calms a Storm

On that day, when evening had come, he said to them, "Let us go across to the other side." And leaving the crowd, they took him with them in the boat, just as he was. And other boats were with him. And a great windstorm arose, and the waves were breaking into the boat, so that the boat was already filling. But he was in the stern, asleep on the cushion. And they woke him and said to him, "Teacher, do you not care that we are perishing?" And he awoke and rebuked the wind and said to the sea, "Peace! Be still!" And the wind ceased, and there was a great calm. He said to them, "Why are you so afraid? Have you still no faith?"

Mark 4:35-40

This quotation from the Bible describes the main purpose of the devotional before you. Having faith helps us to stay calm and be at peace in all circumstances. Most of us do not have a faith strong enough to accomplish this. My hope is that by studying a relevant Bible verse every day that has to do with not fearing, not worrying and being strong and courageous, your faith may increase. That is what has been happening to me as I have worked on this manuscript. The rest of this introduction describes how I came to create this devotional.

In the small Nixon Chapel First Methodist Church in rural Alabama, the preacher was saying that the expression "Fear not," was in the Bible 365 times. That is one fear not for every day of the year. That got my attention.

"Wow," I thought, "That's incredible. God did that. He gave me one *fear not* for every day. That means I never have to be afraid." That concept excited me.

I also thought that 365 Bible verses with the words "Fear not" would be a good idea for a daily devotional. You could have it on your desk at work and look at a verse each day. You could face the day with courage.

A few weeks later, I was having lunch in Kentucky Fried Chicken with some of my tennis friends. We had played our usual Tuesday morning matches and were now relaxing with the buffet and fellowship. We often discuss biblical concepts. It's better than gossiping. I mentioned the sermon about "Fear not" being in the Bible 365 times. Again I started thinking about the idea for a devotional. I shared my idea with three friends. At that moment I decided that I would write it. The thought just popped into my head. I asked these three others to hold me accountable. They agreed. They didn't say they wouldn't. I think I was the only one that was very excited about the idea.

I was 68 years old at the time. I always had a dream of being a writer. When I started college, I was a creative writing major. That changed and to be practical, I graduated with a degree in English and Special Education. Through the years, I've written a few short stories and poems. They are put away in a file cabinet. I've kept journals on and off. They are in that same cabinet. I've read lots of books. However, now I am going to be a writer.

I researched the subject and discovered that the statement about "Fear not," being in the Bible 365 times is not true. There was a football movie where the coach told that to his players. It has become a kind of Bible legend. My internet search told me there would be more than 365 verses if you count things like, "Do not be troubled, do not worry, be brave, stand firm, have courage, etc."

We all know that the internet is not the most reliable source. I decided to read the Bible from beginning to end and see for myself how many relevant verses I could find. I would start on January 1, 2016. My goal was to finish by the end of the year.

As the year progressed and my Bible reading continued, I learned much about what God has to say and what he expects from his people. I saw that the Bible is very relevant today. My faith was increasing. My fears were decreasing. I realized that this might actually be a meaningful book that could help people. In my opinion, this is the insecure planet.

We all have so many insecurities. Most people spend a lot of time worrying. A woman in my Bible study class several years ago shared a philosophy from her mother. Her mother always said, "If you are going to pray, don't worry. If you are going to worry, don't pray. So you might as well pray." That is great wisdom. It is not that easy for most. This book might help people with many common fears. In reading the Bible and working on this devotional, I have learned that God truly demands that we have faith in Him and do not be afraid.

Everyone, including me, has their own set of fears. Some of the most common are snakes, dentists, public speaking, worries about money, worries about loved one's health and safety, violence and terror attacks. This book is not meant to cure severe anxiety disorders or phobias. It might help some people to feel more courageous and less fearful on a daily basis.

Fear Not

Many years ago, I had a friend who was always saying to me, "Aren't you afraid." I got tired of hearing that. That year my New Year's resolution was to remove the words "fear" and "afraid" from my vocabulary. The next time she said, "Aren't you afraid?" I said, "I don't know what that word means." That might not have been very nice, but we both started acting with a little more courage. Then when I was nearly done with this book, my husband said, "You know if a snake runs in front of you, you are going to scream. You will be afraid." He is right. We take small steps.

Finally, I would like to address the fact that this book is based on the Old and New Testament of the Bible. Verses quoted are taken mostly from the English Standard Version translation. If other translations are used, it is noted. I have not tried to interpret the Bible. I am not a biblical scholar. Nor am I a preacher. The relevant verses are listed in chronological order, starting with Genesis and ending with Revelations. I offer a brief explanation as to the context of the verse. The verse is quoted in italics. Next, there is a short prayer. It is my prayer. All I am offering is what I felt led to offer to the Lord in prayer after reading the verse. If you are using this devotional, my prayer may be a guide to you. You may have your own prayer. I pray that this book will be a benefit to those who read it. Writing it has benefitted me. It has taken a year of study and prayer to create. If one person finds comfort in the Lord as a replacement for fear, that will be a blessing.

Fear Not

January 1

The Lord is speaking to Abram.

"Fear Not Abram, I am your shield; your reward shall be very great"

Genesis 15:1

Dear LORD, help me to go into this New Year bravely, knowing that you are my shield. Shield me from all the evils of this world. I praise you and thank you, LORD. Amen.

Fear Not

January 2

God is speaking to Abraham.

But God said to Abraham, "Don't be worried about the boy and your slave Hagar…"

Genesis 21-12 GNT

Dear Lord, at times things do not go the way I plan, but you have a plan. Your plan is always the correct plan. Help me remember to pray instead of worrying. I thank you for being in control. Amen.

Fear Not

January 3

Abraham sent Hagar and her son Ishmael into the desert with only bread and water. When the water was gone, Hagar was afraid that her son would die. Hagar asked God not to let her watch her son die.

And God heard the voice of the boy, and the angel of God called to Hagar from heaven and said to her, "What troubles you, Hagar? Fear not, for God has heard the voice of the boy where he is…"

Genesis 21:17

Dear Lord, you heard the prayer of Ishmael. I know you hear my prayers. If I have faith, I will have your blessing. Everything will be as it should. I praise you Lord, and thank you for your blessing. Amen.

January 4

God speaks to Isaac.

And the Lord appeared to him the same night and said, "I am the God of Abraham, your father. Fear not, for I will bless you and multiply your offspring for my servant Abraham's sake."

Genesis 26:24

Dear Lord, I know that when I have a fear I can tell it to you. You already know about it. You are there with me and with those for whom I am praying. Be with me. Be with the children. In your will all will be as it should. I praise you Lord, and thank you for your blessing. Amen.

Fear Not

January 5

This is a quote from a midwife speaking to Jacob's wife Rachael. Rachael died giving birth.

"Do not fear, for you have another son."

Genesis 35:17

Dear Lord, help us all in times of suffering. Life is filled with joy and tragedy. Help us to embrace life when it seems to be at its worst. Praise you Lord, and thank you for everything; the joys and the sorrows. Lord, you are the beginning and the end. You give and you take away. But the best is that your love endures forever. Amen.

January 6

The steward of Joseph's house speaking is speaking to Joseph's brothers, years after they sold him into slavery.

He replied, "Peace to you, do not be afraid. Your God and the god of your father has put treasure in your sacks for you..."

Genesis 43:23

Dear Lord, thank you for providing me with all the treasures in my life. Let me remember that you will give me whatever I need. I need never worry or be afraid. Thank you for the abundance. I praise you, Lord. Amen.

Fear Not

January 7

Joseph is speaking to his brothers.

"...Now don't be worried or angry with yourselves because you sold me here. God sent me here ahead of you to save people's lives."

Genesis 45:5 NCV

Dear Lord, you are so amazing. Even when I am afraid because of the sins I have committed, you will forgive me if I ask. You can use all things for good. I know if I give my problems to you, I will feel better and all will work out according to Your will. I thank you Lord, for being with me and loving me, despite not being perfect. Amen.

Fear Not

January 8

Then Pharaoh said to Joseph, "Tell your brothers, 'Take wagons from the land of Egypt to carry your little children and your wives, and bring your father here. Don't worry about your personal belongings, for the best of all the land of Egypt is yours.'"

Genesis 45:19-20 NLT

Dear Lord, I know that my true riches are in your kingdom. Help me to never worry about all my stuff. It is not important. You are my God. You are important. I praise you. I thank you for the comforts you have given me here on earth, but let me focus on you. I thank you for being such a great inspiration in my life. Amen.

Fear Not

January 9

God spoke to Jacob before he left home to move to a new land.

"... Do not be afraid to go down to Egypt, for there I will make you into a new nation."

Genesis 46:3

Dear Lord, please comfort me on my life's journeys. Protect me as I go. If I go to a new place, a new job, a new venture, be with me and guide me. If you are with me, who can be against me? I will be brave and courageous. I praise you and thank you Lord. Amen.

Fear Not

January 10

Joseph is speaking after the death of his father Jacob. His brothers were afraid he would hold a grudge.

But Joseph said to them, "Do not fear, for am I in the place of God ..."

Genesis 50:19

Dear Lord, please surround me with people who will support, encourage and protect me. Help me to forgive others, as I would like them to forgive me. I thank you. Praise to you God. Amen.

January 11

Joseph continues speaking to his brothers after the death of their father.

"You intended to harm me, but God intended it for good to accomplish what is now being done, and saving of many lives. So then don't be afraid. I will provide for you and your children."

Genesis 50:20, 21 NIV

Dear Lord, help me to remember that at times you use bad things for good. Help me see any suffering or adversity as a blessing. Help me to believe that you will provide. Thank you for always being with me and providing all my needs. I praise you Lord. Amen.

Fear Not

January 12

This was when Moses had led the Israelites into the desert and the Egyptian Pharaoh's army was pursuing. The Israelites complained that Moses led them into the wilderness to die.

"Moses answered the people, "Do not be afraid. Stand firm and you will see the deliverance the Lord will bring you today..."

Exodus 14:13

Dear Lord, please help me to know that I am safe in your presence. Moses went on to say, "The lord will fight for you, and you only have to be silent." Lord, always remind me that I need to give my troubles to you. What a marvelous solution. I praise you, Lord, and thank you for always lightening my burden. Amen.

Fear Not

January 13

This is Moses and the people of Israel singing this song of praise to the Lord.

"The Lord is my strength and my song, and he has become my salvation; this is my God, and I will praise him, my father's God, and I will exalt him."

Exodus 15:2

Dear Lord, Your words say it all. You are my strength. You are my courage. I will not fear. When I feel weak or afraid, you make me strong. I can stand firm in knowing that you are with me. I give you praise. I thank you for my blessings. I thank you for any courage that I possess. Amen.

Fear Not

January 14

This takes place after God speaks to the people from Mt Sinai. The people ask Moses to speak to them but not to let God speak to them. They are afraid they may die.

Moses said to the people, "Do not fear, for God has come to test you, that the fear of him may be before you, that you may not sin."

Exodus 20:20

Dear Lord, please keep me safe and on the right path. Help me do what you would want me to do. I know that if I trust in you, you will keep my path straight. That is the path I choose to follow. Thank you for showing me the way. I give you praise. Your love endures forever. Amen.

Fear Not

January 15

God sent an angel to speak about the laws for the people of Israel while Moses is leading them.

"I will send my terror before you and will throw into confusion all the people against whom you shall come, and I will make all your enemies turn their backs to you."

Exodus 23:27

Dear Lord, you are so mighty. I praise you. In biblical days you protected your people from their enemies. You will do the same today. Let us love our enemies. Let us forgive our enemies as you forgive us. Then let us rest calmly, knowing you are our loving father and our protector. I thank you for being with your people. Amen.

January 16

Moses is speaking to the Israelites as he sent them to explore Canaan.

"... Is the land rich or poor? Are there trees or not? Be courageous and bring back the land's fruit." It was the season of the first ripe grapes.

Numbers 13:20 CEB

Dear Lord, I thank you for the rich harvests. Thank you for the trees and the fruit. You make all things grow. You supply our food. You supply the very air we breathe. Help me be courageous in all that I do. Give me the confidence to share all that I have. Let me be generous in my offerings. You make me strong. I praise you Lord. Amen.

Fear Not

January 17

Joshua was speaking to the people in the desert who were grumbling about Moses and Aaron, their leaders. Joshua had explored Canaan, the land of milk and honey.

"Only do not rebel against the Lord. And do not be afraid of the people of the land because he will swallow them up."

Numbers 14:9 NIV

Dear Lord, help me to know your will and submit to it. Do not allow me to have a rebellious spirit. Show me how to do things your way and not my way. That will give me security. Thank you for being there and keeping me safe in your love. Praise you Lord. Amen.

January 18

This is a continuation of the devotion from Day 17. Joshua is speaking to the grumbling people in the desert.

"...Their protection is gone, but the Lord is with us. Do not be afraid of them."

Numbers 14:9 NIV

Dear Lord, if you are with me, who can come against me. Protect me and everyone dear to me. I thank you and give you praise. I crave your comfort. Your comfort gives me hope and peace. Your love is so valuable to me. I hope I am worthy in returning that love to you. Amen.

Fear Not

January 19

The Lord is speaking to Moses about Og, the king of Bashan.

But the Lord said to Moses, "Do not fear him, for I have given him into your hand, and all his people, and his land. And you shall do to him as you did to Sihon king of the Amorites, who lived at Heshbon."

Numbers 21:34

Dear Lord, I thank for giving me courage. You tell Moses not to be afraid and he had actual dangerous enemies. I will not fear my enemies. Sometimes people fear unknown enemies. I will just keep you with me at all times, and you will keep me safe. I will be in your protection. I will walk in your path. I will always give you praise and thanks. Amen.

Fear Not

January 20

Moses is speaking to the Israelites. After forty years in the desert they are about to enter the promise land. There are now too many people for Moses to govern alone. He has chosen others to assist in leadership. These are his words to the judges he has chosen.

"Do not show partiality in judging; hear both small and great alike. Do not be afraid of any man, for judgment belongs to God. Bring me any case too hard for you, and I will hear it. And at that time I told you everything you were to do."

Deuteronomy 1:17 NIV

Dear Lord, I praise your word. There is great advice in these verses. Moses tells us not to fear any man. God is the judge, not us. He tells us that when something is too difficult for us we can seek godly counsel. I will try to remember this very important advice. I will always try to be just, brave and nonjudgmental. I thank you Lord for these wonderful words of wisdom. Amen.

January 21

Moses is speaking to the Israelites, retelling past events.

"... See the Lord your God has set the land before you. Go up, take possession, as the Lord, the God of your fathers had told you. Do not fear or be dismayed."

Deuteronomy 1:21

Dear Lord, I praise you for the courage you are giving me. When you bring opportunity my way, let me not be afraid to accept it. Let me try new things. Open my eyes and my heart to the gifts you place before me. I thank you Lord. Amen.

Fear Not

January 22

Moses is still speaking to the people of Israel about their forty year journey. He tells of when they were rebellious and fearful about entering the hill country of the Amorites.

Then I said to you, "Do not be in dread or afraid of them. The Lord your God who goes before you will himself fight for you, just as he did for you in Egypt before your eyes, and in the wilderness, where you have seen how the Lord your God carried you, as a man carries his son, all the way that you went until you came to this place."

Deuteronomy 1:29-31

Dear Lord, I praise you. How great you are. How could I be afraid? You are on my side. Where I go, you go. My battles are your battles if I will just give them to you. I will be victorious if I keep you in my life. I thank you for being on my team. Amen.

Fear Not

January 23

Moses is now telling the Israelites what the Lord told him about King Og and entering the land of Bashan.

But the Lord said to me, "Do not fear him, for I have given him and all his people and his land into your hand. And you shall do to him as you did to Sihon the king of the Amorites, who lived at Heshbon."

Deuteronomy 3:2

Dear Lord, you said not to fear. I must try to obey you. I must try my best to always walk in courage. Let me trust you. I praise you. I thank you for your comfort and the security that only you provide. Please watch over our country. I thank you for the fact that I live in a wonderful country. Everything comes from you. Amen.

Fear Not

January 24

The Lord is now speaking to the people of Israel and the kings about the land they are being told to take over.

"You shall not fear them, for it is the Lord your God who fights for you."

Deuteronomy 3:22

Dear Lord, thank you for being on my side. I praise you. I thank you for teaching me through your word to be just. I know if I trust you and follow you, you will fight for me. How can I be afraid of losing any battle with God on my side? Amen.

Fear Not

January 25

Moses is now telling the Israelite the commandment God has given them about entering a new land. The Israelites are concerned that they will face enemies stronger and more powerful.

"you shall not be afraid of them but you shall remember what the Lord your God did to Pharaoh and to all Egypt, the great trials that your eyes saw, the signs, the wonders, the mighty hand, and the outstretched arm, by which the Lord your God brought you out. So will the Lord your God do to all the peoples of whom you are afraid."

Deuteronomy 7:18-19

Dear Lord, I shall not be afraid. That is your command. There may be troubles that seem to be too big to face, but you will be there. I thank you for being there for me. I praise you. Your strength gives me strength. Amen.

January 26

Moses continues with the rules for living given to the Israelites by the Lord.

"When a prophet speaks in the name of the Lord, if the word does not come to pass or come true, that is a word that the Lord has not spoken; the prophet has spoken it presumptuously. You need not be afraid of him."

Deuteronomy 18:22

Dear Lord, I praise you. I thank you for the prophets you have sent to bring us your word. But Lord, please help us to know whose words are true. There are a lot of predictions of bad things that might happen. These predictions can be frightening. Sometimes people claim these are your words. Grant peace to your people. Let them not fear needlessly. Instead we should pray continually. Lord, please continue to bring peace to your people, as I know you will. Amen.

Fear Not

January 27

Moses continues to instruct the Israelites before going into the land God has promised.

"When you go out to war against you enemies, and see horses and chariots and an army larger than you own, you shall not be afraid of them, for the Lord your God is with you, who brought you out of the land of Egypt."

Deuteronomy 20:1

Dear Lord, I praise you. In this world, there are many types of wars, many enemies, and many types of slavery. Help me be a brave warrior in my daily struggles. I know you will give me strength and courage. Thank you for blessing me. Amen.

Fear Not

January 28

Moses continues to instruct the Israelites about entering their new land.

"And when you draw near to the battle, the priest shall come forward and speak to the people and shall say to them, 'Hear, O Israel, today you are drawing near for battle against your enemies: let not your heart faint. Do not fear or panic or be in dread of them, for the Lord your God is he who goes with you to fight for you against your enemies, to give you the victory.'"

Deuteronomy 20:2-4

Dear Lord, please give me the strength and courage to rise up against my enemies. Let my life be filled with your victory. I praise you and thank you. Amen

January 29

Moses continues to instruct the Israelites about entering their new land.

"And the officers shall speak further to the people and say, 'Is there any man who is fearful and fainthearted? Let him go back to his house, lest he make the heart of his fellows melt like his own.'"

Deuteronomy 20:8

Dear Lord, I praise you always and thank you for any peace I have in my life. Sometimes there are very difficult circumstances people have to face. Some things in life can be terrifying. These can only be faced with your courage and wisdom. Our courage can help others. Help me, Lord, in my life to go forward with courage. Help me to be an example to others. Watch over your people and be with them when it seems too hard. Guide the frightened to safety. Amen.

January 30

Moses presents laws to the Israelites for living.

"Remember what Amalek did to you on the way as you came out of Egypt, how he attacked you on the way when you were faint and weary, and cut off your tail, those who were lagging behind you, and he did not fear God. Therefore when the Lord your God has given you rest from all your enemies around you, in the land that the Lord your God is giving you for an inheritance to possess, you shall blot out the memory of Amalek from under heaven; you shall not forget."

Deuteronomy 25:17-19

Dear Lord, I praise you and thank you for giving us rest when we are weary and afraid. You provide shelter and rest for those who love you and follow you. Help me not to dwell on bad things from the past. You saved me and gave me rest. I will remember to be brave and not ever worry about the past. You commanded that. Amen.

January 31

Moses is still talking to the Israelites before they cross into Jordan.

"... Be strong and courageous. Do not fear or be in dread of them, for it is the Lord your God who goes with you. He will not leave you or forsake you."

Deuteronomy 31:6

Dear Lord, I praise you. I thank you for any courage you have given me. Give me continued strength to stand up to any who might come against me. I'm grateful to have you by my side. Please help me to keep you close. Amen.

February 1

The Lord is speaking to Moses on Mount Sinai. He is giving Moses rules for the Israelites when they enter the land the Lord has given them. These are God's instructions to the Israelites for living holy lives.

"Therefore you shall do my statutes and keep my rules and perform them, and then you will dwell in the land securely. The land will yield its fruit, and you will eat your fill and dwell in it securely."

Leviticus 25:18-19

Dear Lord, I thank you for the food and shelter you provide. I praise you for the country of abundance I live in. I know I am your child. I will try to follow your commands and live in a way that is pleasing to you. That is my security. I need not fear. I have an awesome, generous father in heaven watching out for me. Amen.

Fear Not

February 2

Moses continues talking to the Israelites before they cross into Jordan.

"Then Moses summoned Joshua and said to him in sight of all Israel, 'Be strong and courageous, for you shall go with this people into the land that the Lord has sworn to their fathers to give them, and you shall put them in possession of it...'"

Deuteronomy 31:7

Dear Lord, I praise you. I thank you for any courage that I may possess. I can be strong and courageous because you are with me all the time. You protect your people. Lord, I pray it is your will to protect our country in these trying times. Lord, help me to keep you close. You alone make me strong. Amen.

February 3

Moses continues talking to the Israelites before they cross into Jordan.

"... It is the Lord who goes before you. He will be with you; he will not leave you or forsake you. Do not fear or be dismayed."

Deuteronomy 31:8

Dear Lord, I love these words of scripture. What a great comfort to know that you will not leave me or forsake me. I hope I can be trusted to never leave you or forsake you. As long as I remain by you, I will not fear or be troubled. I will give my troubles to you. Lord, I thank you for your constant love. Amen.

Fear Not

February 4

Moses continues talking to the Israelites before they cross into Jordan.

"And the Lord commissioned Joshua the son of Nun and said, 'Be strong and courageous, for you shall bring the people of Israel into the land that I swore to give them. I will be with you.'"

Deuteronomy 31:23

Dear Lord, help me to be strong and courageous at all times for you are with me always. I thank you for everything in my life, and especially for your constant companionship. When I face new things, or go to new, unfamiliar places that might cause some people anxiety, I know you are by my side guiding me. That gives me courage. I am not afraid. I praise your name. Amen.

Fear Not

February 5

Moses has died and the Lord is now speaking to Joshua.

"No man shall be able to stand before you all the days of your life. Just as I was with Moses, so I will be with you. I will not leave you or forsake you. Be strong and courageous, for you shall cause this people to inherit the land that I swore to their fathers to give them."

Joshua 1:5-6

Dear Lord, please give me strength and courage to go forward and do what needs to be done. I thank you Lord. Amen.

Fear Not

February 6

The Lord is speaking to Joshua.

"Only be strong and very courageous, being careful to do according to all the law that Moses my servant commanded you. Do not turn from it to the right hand or to the left, that you may have good success wherever you go."

Joshua 1:7

Dear Lord, please help me with this. Being strong and courageous is your command. Help me to trust in you and walk straight on the path you have set out for me. Only you can keep me on that straight path and allow me to walk with only strength and courage. I am leaning on you as I go ahead in my life. I praise you and thank you for staying close to me. Amen.

February 7

The Lord is speaking to Joshua.

"Have I not commanded you? Be strong and courageous."

Joshua 1:9

Dear Lord, help me to understand that my courage is not a suggestion, but a command from your mouth. Thank you for your strength. I praise you for letting me share in it. Amen.

Fear Not

February 8

The Lord continues speaking to Joshua. This is a continuation of Joshua 1:9.

"... Do not be frightened, and do not be dismayed, for the Lord your God is with you wherever you go."

Joshua 1:9

Dear Lord, I am starting to understand that I must not fear. You are always walking beside me. I praise you and thank you. Amen.

February 9

The Lord is speaking to Joshua before going into another new land.

"And the Lord said to Joshua, "Do not fear and do not be dismayed..."

Joshua 8:1

Dear Lord, help me to be brave and joyous. Let me be thankful for all things. The world is unpredictable, but you remain constant and faithful. I praise you, Lord. Amen.

Fear Not

February 10

The Lord is speaking to Joshua as he goes into battle.

"And the Lord said to Joshua, 'Do not fear them, for I have given them into your hands. Not a man of them shall stand before you.'"

Joshua 10:8

Dear Lord, I will not fear my enemies. When my country fights battles, may you be with the men and women who fight. May you also bless the men and women at home who engineer the instruments of war, who work in the factories, and all who support our military. Other enemies attacking me may be disease, depression, terrorism at home, poverty, and injustice. I praise you, Lord, for protecting me. I thank you for the courage you give me. Amen.

Fear Not

February 11

Joshua encourages his men in battle.

"And Joshua said to them, 'Do not be afraid or dismayed; be strong and courageous. For thus the Lord will do to all your enemies against whom you fight.'"

Joshua 10:25

Dear Lord, Joshua has said it all. Help me be strong and courageous. Help me to live the life you want for me. I thank you, Lord. Amen.

Fear Not

February 12

Now kings from all over are planning to attack the Israelites.

"And the Lord said to Joshua, 'Do not be afraid of them, for tomorrow at this time I will give over all of them, slain, to Israel…'"

Joshua 11:6

Dear Lord, I thank you for always being there for me. You are my strength. I give praise and thanks to you Lord. Because of you, there is not one that I need fear. Amen.

Fear Not

February 13

Joshua is old now and he is saying farewell to the leaders of the Israelites after some years of peace.

"Be ye therefore very courageous to keep and to do all that is written in the Book of the Law of Moses, that ye turn not aside therefrom to the right hand or to the left;"

Joshua 23:6 KJV

Dear Lord, I need your help always to be very brave. We all need help in keeping your commands. Help to keep my path straight. Do not let me stray or wander from the path you want me to follow. I praise you and thank you, Lord, for giving me direction in my life. Amen.

February 14

Jael, the wife of Heber the Kenite, is speaking to Sisera. This occurs during the period when Deborah rules as Judge. There is much warfare and espionage at this time.

"And Jael came out to meet Sisera and said to him, 'Turn aside, my lord; turn aside to me; do not be afraid.' So he turned aside to her into the tent, and she covered him with a rug."

Judges 4:18

Dear Lord, I praise you. Help me to be brave. Also, help me to know whom to trust in this world. I know I can trust you. People, however, are not always to be trusted, and I need your wisdom to know whom else I should trust. If I trust your guidance, then I will have the confidence to go forward securely. Cover me with your love. Amen.

Fear Not

February 15

God is speaking to the Israelites through an unnamed prophet.

"... And I said to you, 'I am the LORD your God; you shall not fear the gods of the Amorites in whose land you dwell.' But you have not obeyed my voice."

Judges 6:10

Dear Lord, today I am having trouble voicing my prayer to you. The words are not coming, but you know me, and you know my heart. I know I should only fear you. I should not fear other Gods. The other Gods could be work, or money or other people. Stay with me, Lord. Amen.

Fear Not

February 16

Gideon has asked for a sign. Then he saw an angel of God face to face.

"But the Lord said to him, 'Peace be to you. Do not fear; you shall not die.'"

Judges 6:23

Dear Lord, remind me of your importance when I am upset over small things. I thank you, Lord, for your peace. What a blessing! You are what is important. Amen.

February 17

The Lord is speaking to Gideon.

"... Now therefore proclaim in the ears of the people, saying, 'Whoever is fearful and trembling, let him return home and hurry away from Mount Gilead.'"

Judges 7:3 ESV

Dear Lord, please help me to continue following you. If the path gets difficult, still let me persevere. I do not want to be too timid to go where you lead me. Help me to have faith. Then I know you will lead me with strength and confidence. I praise you and thank you for keeping me moving forward in courage. Amen.

Fear Not

February 18

The Lord continues speaking to Gideon.

"That same night the Lord said to him, 'Arise, go down against the camp, for I have given it into our hand. But if you are afraid to go down, go down to the camp with Purah your servant. And you shall hear what they say, and afterward your hands shall be strengthened to go down against the camp.'"

Judges 7:9-11

Dear Lord, at times I am not as strong as I would like to be. Then I know you will surround me with people who can offer me support. Let me not be too proud to ask for help. Let me always remember that you are watching over me and you will provide a way for me. I praise you and thank you, Lord. Amen.

February 19

Boaz is speaking to Ruth.

"And now, my daughter, do not fear. I will do for you all that you ask, for all my fellow townsmen know that you are a worthy woman."

Ruth 3:11

Dear Lord, I thank you for all my blessings. Let me continue to live the life that you have planned for me. Help me to please you in all I do. Make my life worthy. In doing this, I know that you will watch over me. I will be safe. I never need to fear. Amen.

Fear Not

February 20

Hannah is crying in grief because she is barren. She has promised if the Lord would give her a son she would dedicate him to the Lord. Eli sees her and she tells him of her grief.

"Then Eli answered, 'Go in peace, and the God of Israel grant your petition that you have made to him.' And she said, 'Let your servant find favor in your eyes.' Then the woman went her way and ate, and her face was no longer sad."

1 Samuel 1:17-18

Dear Lord, today I have been inspired to offer a special prayer. I want to give everything to you. I will give you all my trouble. I will give you all my problems. I am giving you the gift of my faith. Then I will fill my heart with joy, and I believe that will please you. I thank you for everything in my life. Help me keep that faith as I praise you. Amen.

Fear Not

February 21

This is Hannah's prayer for her infant son, Samuel, as she dedicates him to the Lord.

"The bows of the mighty are broken, but the feeble bind on strength."

1 Samuel 2:4

Dear Lord, I have come to understand that there is often strength in weakness. Often we are most courageous when broken. Lord, help me to know that even when I feel the most vulnerable, that is when my strength may shine through. This world is a difficult place in which to live. Give me courage and strength. I praise you and thank you in advance for this. Amen.

Fear Not

February 22

Eli's daughter-in-law is giving birth at the time that Israel has experienced incredible losses in battle.

"And about the time of her death the women attending her said to her, 'Do not be afraid, for you have borne a son.' But she did not answer or pay attention."

1 Samuel 4:20

Dear Lord, can you give us courage in the most terrible circumstances? I believe you can. This verse is troubling. Things like this still happen today. A child is born. A mother dies. That is your will, and only you know why. As hard as it is, let us give thanks for all things. Give us courage when we need it most. Amen.

Fear Not

February 23

Saul is searching for his father's lost donkeys. He goes to see Samuel, the prophet. God has previously spoken to Samuel about Saul.

"I am the seer," Samuel replied. "Go up ahead of me to the high place, for today you are to eat with me, and in the morning I will let you go and will tell you all that is in your heart. As for the donkeys you lost three days ago, do not worry about them; they have been found. And to whom is all the desire of Israel turned, if not to you and all your father's family line?"

1 Samuel 9:19-20 NIV

Dear Lord, you have told me many times not to worry about my possessions. You told me to fear not. Please help me to obey you. You are aware of any problem I have. You already have a solution. I will trust in your plans, not mine. I thank you, Lord, for being in control. I praise you. Amen.

February 24

Samuel is giving his farewell speech to the Israelites.

"Then the Lord sent Jeerub-Baal, Barak, Jephthah and Samuel, and he delivered you from the hands of your enemies on every side, so that you lived in safety."

1 Samuel 12:11 NIV

Dear Lord, you alone are my security. Today people want insurance policies. Some trust the police or the government. Some look to their families for security. You are who I will always look to for my safety. Then I need not be afraid. Please continue to give me comfort, Lord. Remind me always to keep you close. I thank you for everything in my life, and I praise you always. Amen.

Fear Not

February 25

Samuel is giving his farewell address to the Israelites. He is referring to when they asked for a king.

"And Samuel said to the people, 'Do not be afraid; you have done all this evil. Yet do not turn aside from following the LORD, but serve the LORD with all your heart...'"

1 Samuel 12:20

Dear Lord, help me to serve you with all my heart. Remind me that you alone are my safety. I thank you, Lord, and praise you. Amen.

February 26

Samuel continues his farewell speech to the Israelites.

"Only fear the LORD and serve him faithfully with all your heart. For consider what great things he has done for you."

1 Samuel 12:24

Dear Lord, I praise you and thank you always. This Bible verse tells me only to fear the Lord. To me, that means fear nothing else. God wanted the Israelites to fear no other gods. I will fear nothing of this world. I will not worry about money, my family's health, or my future. It is all in your hands. We are in your safe keeping. I will only trust in you. Amen.

Fear Not

February 27

Jonathan is speaking to David. David fears for his life.

And Jonathan said, "Far be it from you! If I knew that it was determined by my father that harm should come to you, would I not tell you?"

1 Samuel 20:9

Dear Lord, sometimes I have to trust others. Sometimes I just trust you. Give me the wisdom to know when I am with righteous people who will treat me with justice and respect. In other words, Lord, please have my back. Watch over me. I trust you to do that. I praise you and thank you. With you, I need not fear. Amen.

February 28

David is speaking to Abiathar, the priest, about Saul trying to kill him.

"... Stay with me; do not be afraid, for he who seeks my life seeks your life. With me you shall be in safekeeping."

1 Samuel 22:23

Dear Lord, stay with me. With you, I will be safe. I thank you, Lord, for being by my side. I praise you always, Lord. Amen.

February 29

Moses is telling the Israelites what the Lord commands of them.

"Love the Lord your God with all your heart and with all your soul and with all your strength. These commandments that I give you today are to be upon your hearts."

Deuteronomy 6:5-6 NIV

Dear Lord, today I picked a different verse, kind of out of order. Today is a special day. It only comes once every four years. The beauty of the mathematical order of your universe causes this day. So I just chose a special, favorite verse that sums up how I want to live and trust you totally, so that I can always be confident and never be afraid. I thank you, Lord, for all my days, including this extra one. Amen.

March 1

Jonathan went to David and strengthened his hand in God.

"And he said to him, 'Do not fear, for the hand of Saul my father shall not find you. You shall be king over Israel, and I shall be next to you. Saul my father also knows this.'"

1 Samuel 23:17

Dear Lord, your hand gives me strength. I do not need to be afraid. Thank you for your courage. Thank you for your never ending love. I praise you. Amen.

March 2

Saul is afraid of the army of Philistines. He prays to God and gets no answer. Saul has not obeyed all God has ordered of him. Saul gets no answer from God. Therefore he goes to see a woman who can see spirits and talk to the dead. He asks her to bring up Samuel, the dead king.

The king said to her, "Do not be afraid. What do you see?" And the woman said to Saul, "I see a god coming up out of the earth."

1 Samuel 28:13

Dear Lord, help me always to obey your wishes. I know you are always close. I truly hope you are pleased with the choices and decisions I make. I hope my life is pleasing to you. I thank you for being my guide. I praise you, Lord. Amen.

March 3

David is speaking to Mephibosheth, the physically handicapped son of Jonathan and grandson of Saul. David chooses Mephibosheth to be given land, prosperity, and favor with the king.

And David said to him, "Do not fear, for I will show you kindness for the sake of your father Jonathan and I will restore to you all the land of Saul your father, and you shall eat at my table always."

2 Samuel 9:7

Dear Lord, help me to trust our leaders and pray that with your guidance we will be safe. Please keep me under your protection. Watch over our land and our people. You have blessed us with a great nation. Help our leaders follow your will. Amen.

March 4

Joab is speaking to commanders of troops who are surrounded by various enemy warriors.

"Be of good courage, and let us be courageous for our people, and for the cities of God, and may the Lord do what seems good to him."

2 Samuel 10:12

Dear Lord, when trouble surrounds me, you will be there. When danger comes, you will give me courage. I will not be afraid. I will continue to thank you and praise your name. Amen.

March 5

This verse is spoken by Absalom, King David's son, as he is commanding his servants to kill his brother.

Then Absalom commanded his servants, "Mark when Amnon's heart is merry with wine, and when I say to you, 'Strike Amnon,' then kill him. Do not fear; have I not commanded you? Be courageous and be valiant."

2 Samuel 13:28

Dear Lord, I know that sometimes being fearless can lead to trouble. Please in your greatness help me to know your will. Keep my path straight. Help me combine courage with wisdom. I give you all the power to keep me righteous and safe. Thank you for your love and your care. Amen.

March 6

David spoke to the Lord the words of this song on the day when the Lord delivered him from the hand of all his enemies, and from the hand of Saul.

"This God is my strong refuge and has made my way blameless."

2 Samuel 22:33

Dear Lord, you alone give me strength and security. Nothing of the world can offer that to me. For that, I will always praise you. You are my rock. My strength and courage comes from you. It is stronger than what this world can give me. I try to have no enemies, but if someone should come against me, you stand with me. You can turn away their anger. You can give me words of peace. I praise you, Lord, and thank you for everything. Amen.

Fear Not

March 7

David spoke to the Lord the words of this song on the day when the Lord delivered him from the hand of all his enemies, and from the hand of Saul.

"For you equipped me with strength for the battle; you made those who rise against me sink under me."

2 Samuel 22:40

Dear Lord, I praise you. You give me a life worth living. Some days, life feels like a battle. When that happens, you give me the strength to have a good attitude and turn a bad day into a good day. When fear tries to take hold of me, and I do not want to face the people and the events facing me, you go before me and raise me above the situation. With you beside me, I can face anything that comes my way. Amen.

March 8

Elijah is speaking to a widow at Zarephath. God told him to go to her for food and water. But she has hardly any food, and no bread prepared. She and her son are starving and she is preparing to make bread out of the last of their supplies.

"And Elijah said to her, 'Do not fear; go and do as you have said. But first make me a little cake of it and bring it to me, and afterward make something for yourself and your son. For thus says the Lord, the God of Israel, The jar of flour shall not be spent, and the jug of oil shall not be empty, until the day that the Lord sends rain upon the earth.'"

1 Kings 17:13-14

Dear Lord, I thank you, Lord, for your provisions. Help me always to know that you will provide for my needs on time and in abundance. Remind me to never worry about money. I praise you Lord for the bounty you provide. Amen.

March 9

The angel of the Lord is speaking to Elijah.

"Then the angel of the Lord said to Elijah, 'Go down with him; do not be afraid of him.' So he arose and went down with him to the king."

2 Kings 1:15

Dear Lord, when I am afraid of facing anyone, I will remember the words of the Angel of the Lord. "Do not be afraid." I thank you, Lord, for your never ending love and support. You are my courage. Amen.

Fear Not

March 10

Elijah is speaking as the Syrian army is surrounding him and his servants.

"He said, 'Do not be afraid, for those who are with us are more than those who are with them.'"

2 Kings 6:16

Dear Lord, as I go on my way, please let all your heavenly angels surround my loved ones and me. Protect us from all evil and fill our lives with grace. Thank you for the wonderful gifts you have already given us. I praise you with all my heart. Amen.

March 11

This is a little different. Samaria is resettled and God's chosen people are worshipping other gods as well as the Lord.

"The Lord made a covenant with them and commanded them, 'You shall not fear other gods or bow yourselves to them or serve them or sacrifice to them, but you shall fear the Lord, who brought you out of the land of Egypt with great power and with an outstretched arm. You shall bow yourselves to him, and to him you shall sacrifice...'"

2 Kings 17:35-36

Dear Lord, help me to remember that you are the only Lord. Money, power, football, horses, career, or success: these things are not God. Let me never fear losing money, losing at sports, losing pets or jobs. May I always try to listen to you, Lord. I know that you alone are God. You alone keep me safe. Amen.

Fear Not

March 12

This continues the warning to the people of Samaria to only fear one God.

"... And the statutes and the rules and the law and the commandment that he wrote for you, you shall always be careful to do. You shall not fear other gods, and you shall not forget the covenant that I have made with you. You shall not fear other gods, but you shall fear the Lord your God, and he will deliver you out of the hand of all your enemies."

2 Kings 17:37-39

Dear Lord, continue to keep me faithful only to you. I will fear you and nothing else. Only you will keep me safe. You will not let my enemies defeat me, whether the enemies are real or in my mind. You give me security and peace. Without you, I cannot have this safety. I thank you for your comfort. Amen.

March 13

The prophet Isaiah is speaking to King Hezekiah's officials.

"Isaiah said to them, 'Say to your master, Thus says the Lord: Do not be afraid because of the words that you have heard, with which the servants of the king of Assyria have reviled me…'"

2 Kings 19:6

Dear Lord, when the media is so filled with stories of terror, remind me not to be afraid because of their words. When my friends and associates tell me tales of terror, help me not to let their words distress me. Give me the grace to turn away from words that are not encouraging. Thank you for helping me live with courage and awe for you. Amen.

March 14

A Governor, Gedaliah, swore to his men that everything would be well. It wasn't.

"And Gedaliah swore to them and their men, saying, 'Do not be afraid because of the Chaldean officials. Live in the land and serve the king of Babylon, and it shall be well with you.'"

2 Kings 25:24

Dear Lord, sometimes trials come our way. Sometimes there is pain, suffering, hardship and even death. Fears I couldn't conquer prompted me to write this book. I have been counseled that when faced with grave illness or danger, all outcomes will be good. One will either survive or die and be with God. Both outcomes are good. Help me to embrace this and always to find something to be grateful for. Give me the courage to face whatever life throws at me. Life may not work out the way I want. My prayers may not be answered as I hoped. But I know that you, our Lord, are in control. You are my comfort. I will always praise and worship you. Amen.

March 15

David offers a Psalm of Thanks to the Lord before the ark of the covenant of God.

"Seek the Lord and his strength; seek his presence continually."

1 Chronicles 16:11

Dear Lord, I praise you with all my heart. It is mostly good to come to you with no requests. You know my need. You know what is in my heart. It is wonderful just to spend time adoring you. I always want you with me. I want to remember to thank you continually for any and all blessings. You are the most important thing in my life. I hope I can continually seek to be closer to you. Amen.

March 16

David offers a Psalm of Thanks to the Lord before the ark of the covenant of God.

"For all the gods of the peoples are worthless idols, but the Lord made the heavens. Splendor and majesty are before him; strength and joy are in his place. Ascribe to the Lord, O families of the peoples, ascribe to the Lord glory and strength! Ascribe to the LORD the glory due his name; bring an offering and come before him! Worship the Lord in splendor and holiness; tremble before him, all the earth; yes, the world is established; it shall never be moved."

1 Chronicles 16:26-30

Dear Lord, I can only sing praise for your majesty. Your creations are spectacular. I know no words to describe how mighty and wonderful you are. I want to know you in all your glory. I am always so grateful to you. Amen.

March 17

Joab is giving instructions to his troops as they advance against the Arameans and the Ammonties.

"... Be strong and let us fight bravely for our people and the cities of God. The Lord will do what is good in his sight."

1 Chronicles 19:13 NIV

Dear Lord, I know I have battles to fight in my life. I try my best to get along with everyone and always be peaceful. But I have learned that showing that I have the strength and I am not afraid often helps to secure that peace I seek. Help me to use your wisdom in any daily struggle. Help me to do what is right. I trust that you, Lord, control everything in my life, and all is good. I praise you and thank you for your love. Amen.

March 18

King David is speaking to his son Solomon about building a house of the Lord.

"Then you will prosper if you are careful to observe the statutes and the rules that the Lord commanded Moses for Israel. Be strong and courageous. Fear not; do not be dismayed."

1 Chronicles 22:13

Dear Lord, you have been so great in my life. I praise you for all the gifts you have given me. Help me to obey your commands. Help me to listen to you. Allow me to be strong and courageous, knowing that I am walking with you. With you by my side, I will fear not. Thank you, Lord. Amen.

March 19

King David is speaking to his son Solomon about building a house of the Lord.

"Then David said to Solomon his son, 'Be strong and courageous and do it. Do not be afraid and do not be dismayed, for the Lord God, even my God, is with you. He will not leave you or forsake you, until all the work for the service of the house of the Lord is finished...'"

1 Chronicles 28:20

Dear Lord, I praise you. I am brave because I know you are with me. You will not leave me nor forsake me. Let me do your work here on earth and know that I cannot fail. I thank you for blessing me and being by my side. Amen.

March 20

David is praising the Lord to the assembly as he blesses the newly built house of the Lord.

"Both riches and honor come from you, and you rule over all. In your hand are power and might, and in your hand it is to make great and to give strength to all."

1 Chronicles 29:12

Dear Lord, as David praises you, so do I. You are the greatness and power that we men have here on earth. All strength comes from you. You are the source of everything good. You supply it all. Thank you for the abundance. Amen.

March 21

Azariah is prophesying to Asa.

"... But you, take courage! Do not let your hands be weak, for your work shall be rewarded."

2 Chronicles 15:7

Dear Lord, give me courage. Bless the work of my hands. Help me to always act in a way that reflects your goodness and love. You alone are my Lord. I will worship only you and turn to you for making decisions in my life. I praise you, Lord, for I know that your love endures forever. I thank you for your blessings. Amen.

March 22

Azariah has been prophesizing to Asa. Asa responds.

"As soon as Asa heard these words, the prophesy of Azariah the son of Oded, he took courage and put away the detestable idols from all the land of Judah and Benjamin and from the cities that he had taken in the hill country of Ephraim, and he repaired the altar of the Lord that was in front of the vestibule of the house of the Lord."

2 Chronicles 15:8

Dear Lord, you are the only God. You must always be the most important thing in my life. I will always try to put you first. Nothing should ever come before you. That means I put you before my family, before my job, and most certainly before my possessions. Doing this is not always easy to do. But you give me the courage, and then you reward me with peace that transcends anything here on earth. Amen.

March 23

Jehoshaphat is giving instructions to newly appointed judges of Judah.

"... And behold, Amariah the chief priest is over you in all matters of the Lord; and Zebadiah the son of Ishmael, the governor of the house of Judah, in all the king's matters, and the Levites will serve you as officers. Deal courageously, and may the Lord be with the upright!"

2 Chronicles 19:11

Dear Lord, I praise you, and I thank you. Life is full of hard decisions. Help me to always act with courage. I will try to live a righteous life. I know that if I try my best to follow principals spelled out in the Bible, I will do the right thing and the Lord will be with me. I will try to be brave in making decisions. You will be my helper. Amen.

March 24

The spirit of the Lord is speaking to the people of Judah and Jehoshaphat as vast enemy armies are approaching.

"And he said, 'Listen, all Judah and inhabitants of Jerusalem and King Jehoshaphat: Thus says the Lord to you, Do not be afraid and do not be dismayed at this great horde, for the battle is not yours but God's...'"

2 Chronicles 20:15

Dear Lord, sometimes I feel that the world around me is spinning out of control. Help me to know that sometimes I need to give the battle to you. I can give problems to you, Lord, when they feel too big for me. Your love endures forever. Your strength is unlimited. I praise you. I thank you for your blessings and your protection. Amen.

March 25

The spirit of the Lord continues speaking to the people of Judah and Jehoshaphat as vast enemy armies are approaching.

"... You will not need to fight in this battle. Stand firm, hold your position, and see the salvation of the Lord on your behalf, O Judah and Jerusalem.' Do not be afraid and do not be dismayed. Tomorrow go out against them, and the Lord will be with you."

2 Chronicles 20:17

Dear Lord, I am faced with a trial today. Please hear my bedtime prayers. In the morning, may I awake and see without a doubt that you are with me, and all will be according to your will. Thank you for the wisdom to rest in your love and protection. Remind me that in time problems often resolve themselves. With you by my side, and a good night's sleep, I can face whatever comes my way with courage. I praise you and thank you for your constant love. Amen.

March 26

Hezekiah is speaking to his men and the people of Judah.

"Be strong and courageous. Do not be afraid or dismayed before the king of Assyria and all the horde that is with him, for there are more with us than with him. With him is an arm of flesh, but with us is the Lord our God, to help us and to fight our battles. And the people took confidence from the words."

2 Chronicles 32:7-8

Dear Lord, your words give me strength and courage. Your spirit is much more powerful than my flesh. I thank you for being by my side. I can be brave and strong. You go before me, you are on both sides to make it easier to go through a narrow, difficult path, and you cover me from behind. Your protection is complete. I fear nothing. I praise you. Amen.

March 27

Ezra reacts when the Israelites gain permission to live and worship their God in Jerusalem.

"Blessed be the Lord, the God of our fathers, who put such a thing as this into the heart of the king, to beautify the house of the Lord that is in Jerusalem, and who extended to me his steadfast love before the king and his counselors, and before all the king's mighty officers. I took courage, for the hand of the Lord my God was on me, and I gathered leading men from Israel to go up with me."

Ezra 7:27-28

Dear Lord, I praise you and thank you. Often we need not ask for courage in prayers. It is enough to sing your praise. In 2 Chronicles 20:21 the soldiers cry, Give thanks to the Lord, for his steadfast love endures forever. That was enough. They won the battle. Amen.

March 28

Shecaniah tells Ezra that the people must repent for disobeying one of God's commands. It will involve difficult decisions.

"...Rise up; this matter is in your hands. We will support you, so take courage and do it."

Ezra 10:4 NIV

Dear Lord, doing the right thing is not always easy. If we have not always lived according to your commands, it is difficult to undo a poor choice. It is not always possible to make amends. Apologies are not always enough. But you are with us. You bless us. You love us. Help us all Lord to live a Godly life and forgive us our sins. Help us slowly build the best lives we can. I praise you and thank you for your enduring love. Amen.

March 29

Nehemiah is speaking about rebuilding the walls of Jerusalem.

"And I looked and arose and said to the nobles and to the officials and to the rest of the people, 'Do not be afraid of them. Remember the Lord, who is great and awesome, and fight for your brothers, your sons, your daughters, your wives, and your homes.'"

Nehemiah 4:14

Dear Lord, you are great and awesome. I will not fear my enemies. I will rest in the knowledge that I can only protect my loved ones with your help. Help me to walk in your ways, and to please you. I thank you for giving me faith and courage. Amen.

Fear Not

March 30

Nehemiah responds to pressure trying to stop the building of the walls of Jerusalem.

"For they all wanted to frighten us, thinking, 'Their hands will drop from the work, and it will not be done.' But now, O God, strengthen my hands."

Nehemiah 6:9

Dear Lord, give me strength. When I am weary, lift me up. If a task seems too difficult, help me to find a way. There are many kinds of strength; inner strength; outer strength. Some people have strong bodies. Others have strong minds. We can all strengthen our minds and bodies with your help. Our minds and bodies belong to you. Our strong will comes from you. Give us wisdom. Send others to help us when necessary. You are in control. I thank you and praise you for this. Amen.

March 31

Nehemiah is responding to threats against his life.

"But I said, 'Should such a man as I run away? And what man such as I could go into the temple and live? I will not go in.' And I understood and saw that God had not sent him, but he had pronounced the prophecy against me because Tobiah and Sanballat had hired him. For this purpose he was hired, that I should be afraid and act in this way and sin, and so they could give me a bad name in order to taunt me."

Nehemiah 6:11-13

Dear Lord, what should I do when I fear for my life? Help me remember that there is no death for your believers. We may lose our earthly bodies. Then we will be with you. Believing this is a test of true faith. Let my faith be strong. Then I cannot lose. I need a lot of help from you to have that kind of strength. Please, Lord, be with me unto the end. Amen.

April 1

Nehemiah, the governor, is speaking to the Jewish people in Jerusalem.

"Then he said to them, 'Go your way. Eat the fat and drink sweet wine and send portions to anyone who has nothing ready, for this day is holy to our Lord. And do not be grieved, for the joy of the Lord is your strength.'"

Nehemiah 8:10

Dear Lord, with joy in my heart, I offer praise to you. I will try to always find some joy in my life. Loving you gives me triumph. When I am happy and enjoying a good, joyful, God filled life, I will have all the strength I need. My joy and my strength come from following you. I am thankful to have you with me. I will not fear. Amen.

April 2

Now the Levites are speaking to the Jewish people in Jerusalem.

"So the Levites calmed all the people, saying, 'Be quiet, for this day is holy; do not be grieved.'"

Nehemiah 8:11

Dear Lord, often other people can offer us rest from our anxiety. All days are holy. I will try to spend all of my days with you, Lord. Then in those holy days, I will be calm. I will look to calm, godly leaders to offer my support. Please, Lord, continue to put those people in my path. I am grateful for those in my life who offer me calm courage. Thank you, Lord. I praise you every day. Help me to keep all days holy. Amen.

April 3

After Job is faced with loss, tragedy and disease, he cursed the day he was born. Then one of his friends, Eliphaz, the Temanite, gives him encouragement.

"...You will be protected from the lash of the tongue, and need not fear when destruction comes..."

Job 5:21 NIV

Dear Lord, please guard me against any forces which may bring harm my way. I need not fear evil or wrong doers. I need not fear talk of the destruction of mankind. Lord, you are with me. That is all that matters. Amen.

April 4

After Job is faced with loss, tragedy and disease, he cursed the day he was born. Then one of his friends, Eliphaz, the Temanite, continues to give Job encouragement.

"...You will laugh at destruction and famine, and need not fear the beasts of the earth..."

Job 5:22 NIV

Dear Lord, I need not fear destruction. I need not fear poverty, hunger or death. You are with me. I thank you for every day that I walk on this earth. I thank you for my faith. I praise you for the comfort and courage you give to me. Amen.

April 5

Job is responding to his friend's encouragement.

"There is no arbiter between us, who might lay his hand on us both. Let him take his rod away from me, and let not dread of him terrify me."

Job 9:33-34

Dear Lord, as I walk with you and do my best to obey your laws, I shall not fear you. I have respect for you. I know you are in control of my life. But I trust that your plan for me is the correct plan. I may be put through trials. I may not have things turn out the way I want them to. I will, however, trust you. I praise you and thank you for always being with me. I can always give my burdens to you. Amen.

April 6

Job is responding to his friend's encouragement.

"Then I would speak without fear of him, for I am not so in myself."

Job 9:35

Dear Lord, if I obey your commands and try to follow your will, I never need to be in fear of you. And it follows that I should not fear any but you. Therefore, I shall not fear. That is simple. I know it is easier said than done, but you can help me. I praise you, Lord. I thank you for always being in my life. I know you will help me in my struggle to remain courageous. Amen.

April 7

Another one of Job's friends offers encouragement after Job's terrible trials.

"If iniquity is in your hand, put it far away, and let not injustice dwell in your tents. Surely then you will lift up your face without blemish; you will be secure and will not fear."

Job 11:14-15

Dear Lord, help me always try to obey your commands and keep my heart pure. Make my thoughts and actions as blameless as possible for a human. I know you will help me with this request. I can only do this with your help. I thank you, Lord, for loving me. I praise you, Lord. Amen.

April 8

Job's friend continues to encourage him, throughout his trials.

The word <u>secure</u> can be defined as free from anxiety (www.definitions.com). Being secure is not being afraid.

"...And you will feel secure, because there is hope; you will look around and take your rest in security..."

Job 11:18

Dear Lord, I thank you and praise you for always giving me hope. I will be glad to face each day with which you bless me. I know that there is always hope. You will comfort me through hard times, and be with me while I celebrate the good times. Allow joy to replace fear and worry. Strengthen me emotionally. Let me hold your enduring love in my heart. Amen.

April 9

Job's friend continues to encourage him, throughout his trials.

"... You will lie down, and none will make you afraid; many will court your favor ..."

Job 11:19

Dear Lord, what a blessing it is to be able to rest and sleep and not be afraid. If I worry or feel fearful, I will never get a good night's sleep. Lord, I thank you for allowing me to rest peacefully. With a good night's rest, the world will be better tomorrow. Opportunities will come my way. I praise you, Lord. I thank you, Lord. Amen.

April 10

Job responds to his friends' encouragement.

"...With him are strength and sound wisdom; the deceived and the deceiver are his..."

Job 12:16

Dear Lord, we all belong to you. You are the creator and all powerful one. I belong to you. My enemies belong to you. All strength comes from you. All courage comes from you. Help me to stay close to you when I start feeling overwhelmed by the struggles of this life. Stay with me and help me always to feel you near. I praise you Lord for your wondrous deeds. I thank you for being near. Amen.

April 11

Job continues with his response to his friends' encouragement.

"... Only grant me two things, then I will not hide myself from your face: withdraw your hand far from me, and let not dread of you terrify me ..."

Job 13:20-21

Dear Lord, sometimes the storms come too close, the terror is too real. Those are the times when I need to turn to you automatically. You alone will give me the strength to endure the difficult things in life. You alone can keep me calm during the storm. Shield me when trouble comes my way. Please stay with me even if I try to turn away. I praise you for that. Amen.

April 12

Job is speaking about the wicked and questioning his friends about whether the wicked always suffer.

"... Their houses are safe from fear, and no rod of God is upon them ..."

Job 21:9

Dear Lord, I know that you want me to be a good person. You want me to always turn to you. You want me to trust you as my heavenly Father. I believe that you will keep me safe and help me to prosper. But I have learned in life that sometimes people do not live good lives, and still, they are very successful. You have a plan. I trust in it. I know that the wicked may seem to prosper, but no good will come of their wealth. They may lead content lives, but they do not have the peace that comes from knowing you. I am glad to have you in my life. I will not have envy. I praise you and trust you in all your ways. Amen.

Fear Not

April 13

Elihu is younger than the other friends who have tried in vain to encourage Job. Elihu now feels led by God to speak since his elders have not been successful.

"... Behold, no fear of me need terrify you; my pressure will not be heavy upon you ..."

Job 33:7

Dear Lord, I praise you and thank you for your undying love. I do not like when you correct me. I do not like others to correct me. That is a fault, Lord, and I ask you to remove that fault. Let me not fear hearing when I have done wrong. Also, let me not be afraid to speak when I feel I may have some wisdom to offer others who are suffering. I might make someone unhappy. Someone may be angry with me. Let me use wisdom in speaking. Let me turn to you before I open my mouth. Keep me humble. I know I am not free from sin. No man is. Let your word be my guide. Amen.

April 14

The Lord is speaking to Job. He is referring to Job trusting a wild ox and not trusting the Lord.

"... Will you depend on him because his strength is great, and will you leave to him your labor? ..."

Job 39:11

Dear Lord, I love you, I praise you, I thank you, and I trust you. Trusting you is how I show my faith. I must trust you at all times, not just when things are as I wish. It is in hard times that I need my faith the most. It is amazing how I might trust an airplane to stay in the sky. I trust my car to get me safely to where I want to go. It would be very insulting if I didn't trust you. Please, Lord, keep my faith strong, so I may please you. Amen.

Fear Not

April 15

The Lord is speaking to Job describing how his creatures often can be more fearless than man. Here he is referring to a horse in battle.

"... He paws in the valley and exults in his strength; he goes out to meet the weapons. He laughs at fear and is not dismayed; he does not turn back from the sword ..."

Job 39:21-22

Dear Lord, I praise you and thank you for my faith. I want to come to you as a child with a simple faith. I want to live my live free from worry. I try to watch the animals and learn from them. They work as they often must. They live in the moment. They eat when hungry, they rest when tired, and they seem to know how to stay alive. I will just let you watch over me as I go about my daily business, trusting you alone. Amen.

April 16

The Lord is speaking to Job. The Lord is comparing his power to that of a leviathan, which is a whale or a sea monster.

"... In his neck abides strength, and terror dances before him ..."

Job 41:22

Dear Lord, I praise you. I humble myself before your power. I fear you alone because you are almighty and all powerful. If I entrust myself to you, none can come against me. I cannot fight you. I do not want to fight you. With all my heart I want to join you. I want to be on your team. Allow me that privilege. Please keep me close to you and offer me a touch of your great strength. Amen.

April 17

The Lord is speaking to Job. The Lord is comparing his power to that of a leviathan, which is a whale or a sea monster.

"... When he raises himself up, the mighty are afraid; at the crashing they are beside themselves..."

Job 41:25

Dear Lord, once again you are reminding Job and me of your great power. I will fear you alone. You will keep me safe. There is no force that can match you. I want to stay close to you. I want to please you. Help me with this as I praise you for your love. I thank you for being in my life. I thank you for the blanket of security you offer. Amen.

April 18

The Lord is speaking to Job. The Lord is comparing his power to that of a leviathan, which is a whale or a sea monster.

"... On earth there is not his like, a creature without fear ..."

Job 41:33

Dear Lord, as you speak about the sea monster, I am reminded of your great strength. I am also reminded that you give great strength to many of your creatures. Humans are included. Of course, no creature's strength can compare to yours. I will try to be one of your brave creations. I will, however, try my best always to be humble, and know that even the strength to breathe comes from you. I thank you, Lord, for my life. I thank you for whatever strength and courage you choose to grant me. Amen.

April 19

This is a psalm written by David when he fled from his son, Absalom.

"I will not be afraid of many thousands of people who have set themselves against me all around."

Psalm 3:6

Dear Lord, when it looks like everyone is against me, I know you are for me. You are my protector. You provide strength and comfort. There are no odds you cannot win. With you, all things are possible. I praise you and thank you for the courage you provide. Amen.

April 20

This is A Psalm of David, to be accompanied by string instruments.

"In peace I will both lie down and sleep; for you alone, O Lord, make me dwell in safety."

Psalm 4:8

Dear Lord, in this world, the danger is all around. However, you give me the only security that is true. Even when I know there might be a dangerous storm coming, or I hear about terrible crimes that have been committed near me, I am still able to rest peacefully. As I think about you at bedtime, I can put my worries out of my head. It is you alone who can give me the feeling of security that I need. I praise you and thank you, Lord, for your comfort. Amen.

April 21

This psalm of David is to be accompanied by flute.

"But let all who take refuge in you rejoice; let them ever sing for joy, and spread your protection over them, that those who love your name may exalt in you."

Psalm 5:11

Dear Lord, I love that you spread your protection over all who take refuge in you. You offer your love unconditionally to all who love you and choose to follow you. And it is even greater than your offer of joy. That is why I rejoice in your love. I will always try to love your name and exult in you. What a great gift I am given in return, your protection. I praise you, Lord. Amen.

April 22

David sang this psalm to the Lord when the Lord delivered him from the hand of Saul and the hand of his enemies.

"I love you, O Lord, my strength. The Lord is my rock and my fortress and my deliverer, my God, my rock, in whom I take refuge, my shield, and the horn of my salvation, my stronghold."

Psalm 18:1-2

Dear Lord, David has said it better than I could. His words offer a beautiful praise to you. I can only be grateful for the words of the Psalms that offer so much comfort. These verses say what is on my heart. Amen.

April 23

David sang this psalm to the Lord when the Lord delivered him from the hand of Saul and the hand of his enemies.

"It is God who arms me with strength and makes my way perfect."

Psalm 16:32

Dear Lord, I love reading your Psalms. The songs of David always offer me comfort. When I feel insecure, I can turn to the passages in Psalms and be reminded of the strength you give me, of how powerful you are, and the peace you offer. I praise you as your servant David did. I thank you for your blanket of comfort and peace. Amen.

April 24

David sang this psalm to the Lord when the Lord delivered him from the hand of Saul and the hand of his enemies.

"For you equipped me with strength for the battle; you made those who rise against me sink under me."

Psalm 18:39

Dear Lord, today my enemy is fear. Terrible things are happening in this country and this world. I will battle fear today. I ask you to surround me with peace and let not one be my enemy. I know you can do this. You offer me perfect love. I want nothing else. I will be safe in your arms. I thank you, Lord. Amen.

April 25

This song of David is for the director of music.

"Let the words of my mouth, and the meditation of my heart, be acceptable in thy sight, O Lord, my strength, and my redeemer."

Psalm 19:14 KJV

Dear Lord, some translations of this verse use the word protector instead of redeemer. Some translations use the word rock instead of strength. I like that you are my protector. I like that you are my rock and my strength. I pray as David did that the words of my mouth and the meditations of my heart will be acceptable to you. Then, Lord, you will be my strength, my rock, and my redeemer. As David did so beautifully, I will attempt in my way to sing praise to you. I offer you my continual thanks, Lord. Amen.

April 26

This is another Psalm of David.

"But you, O Lord, be not far off; Oh my Strength, come quickly to help me."

Psalm 22:19 NIV

Dear Lord, my words do not sound as musical as David's, but I have uttered similar words when I was involved in a car crash. A pickup truck hit my small car. As my car was spinning, it continued to be hit. I closed my eyes and asked you, Lord, to comfort me, because I knew I might be seriously injured. There was no time to think. It was a gut reaction. I needed your help desperately. You were there. My car was totaled, but I had no injuries. That was many years ago, but I knew then as I know now, you, God, were not far off. Please continue to stay with me, Lord. I thank you for saving my life many times. I praise you, Lord. Amen.

Fear Not

April 27

A Psalm of David

"Even though I walk through the valley of the shadow of death, I will fear no evil, for you are with me; your rod and your staff, they comfort me."

Psalm 23:4

Dear Lord, I suspect this psalm is one of the most loved and quoted chapters of the Bible. It has comforted millions of people of many faiths throughout the world for thousands of years. No wonder when I feel afraid, I turn to the Twenty Third Psalm. I thank you, Lord, for these beautiful words. If I can fear no evil as death approaches, then I never need fear any evil. Sometimes in fearful situations, I might ask, "What's the worst that could happen?" I could die. But then I can be with a wondrous God. This is where faith plays a big part. I must ask you, Lord, to supply that faith. Amen.

April 28

A Psalm of David.

"Surely goodness and mercy shall follow me all the days of my life, and I shall dwell in the house of the Lord forever."

Psalm 23:6

Dear Lord, again David's words are beautiful. I often just dwell and meditate on all the words of the Twenty Third Psalm. If I can dwell in the house of the Lord forever, what more could I possibly want? Of course, all my needs would be met. I would be safe. So I will keep repeating these verses and believing them. And I do believe that goodness and mercy will follow me for the rest of my life. Now I feel at total peace. I truly am grateful to be in your loving graces, Lord. Amen.

April 29

A Psalm of David

"I always look to you, because you rescue me. I am lonely and troubled. Show that you care and have pity on me. My awful worries keep growing. Rescue me from sadness. See my troubles and misery and forgive my sins."

Psalm 25:15-18 CEV

Dear Lord, worries can be overcoming at times. I need your help to free me from them. As always, Lord, I praise you. I thank you for all the blessings in my life. I know that when I worry, I am sinning against you. I am lacking faith. You are offering me joy. I am offering a fervent prayer for you to forgive me if my faith wavers at times and I start to worry. Only you can free me, Lord. Amen.

Fear Not

April 30

A Psalm of David

"The Lord is my light and my salvation; whom shall I fear? The Lord is the stronghold of my life; of whom shall I be afraid?"

Psalm 27:1

Dear Lord, once again the scriptures speak for me. You are my salvation. You are my light. Let me focus on that light. If I have you, I have everything. I see this over and over again in my everyday life. Sometimes when the world seems so crazy, I have no choice but to trust you completely. If I put your light in the center of my world, it isn't crazy anymore. Of whom shall I be afraid? No one. Of what shall I be afraid? Nothing.

May 1

A Psalm of David

"Though an army encamp against me, my heart shall not fear; though war arise against me, yet I will be confident."

Psalm 27:3

Dear Lord, let me look upon your beauty. Hide me in your shelter in times of trouble. I will seek to see your brightness and your glory. You are my courage. Let me walk in your path. I know you will show yourself to me. Remind me, Lord, to wait on you. Protect me and others who may have enemies coming after them. Your wonder amazes me. I praise you, Lord. I thank you, Lord. Amen.

May 2

A Psalm of David

"Wait for the Lord; be strong, and let your heart take courage; wait for the Lord!"

Psalm 27:14

Dear Lord, grant me patience. I thank you for having given me the patience to have survived this long. I once got a fortune cookie that read, "A spoonful of patience is better than a barrel full of brains." That quote has always stuck with me. Lord, your word has just reminded me of that. If I am sick, I may need time and rest to heal. If my heart is broken, it may need time and rest to heal. Lord, I will give you time to do the works in my life that you have planned. I will wait courageously for you always. Amen.

May 3

A Psalm of David

"The Lord is my strength and my shield; in him my heart trusts, and I am helped; my heart exults, and with my song I give thanks to him."

Psalm 28:7

Dear Lord, again your servant David sings a song with words that express my feelings. You are my strength. You give me courage. With your shield, I am often able not to be afraid. I try hard and you, Lord, help me. As David does, I praise you and thank you for everything in my life. All power comes from you. Amen.

May 4

A Psalm of David

"The Lord is the strength of his people; he is the saving refuge of his anointed. Oh, save your people and bless your heritage! Be their shepherd and carry them forever."

Psalm 28:8-9

Dear Lord, you are my strength. You are my power. You are my courage. I am but a helpless sheep. You are my shepherd. You constantly watch over me. You care for my needs. You make sure I have food. You protect me from my enemies. It is you alone in whom I feel secure. I praise you and thank you for your loving care. Amen.

May 5

A Psalm of David

"May the Lord give strength to his people! May the Lord bless his people with peace!"

Psalm 29:11

Dear Lord, let me continue to be one of your people. Then you will continue to bless me with strength and peace. Security follows. I want nothing else. I praise you and thank you for your continuing presence in my life. Help me to keep my faith strong. Amen.

May 6

A Psalm of David

"Incline your ear to me; rescue me speedily! Be a rock of refuge for me, a strong fortress to save me! For you are my rock and my fortress; and for your name's sake you lead me and guide me; you take me out of the net they have hidden for me, for you are my refuge."

Psalm 31:2-4

Dear Lord, let my words go from my lips to your ears. Be my rock. I mainly need you to guide me, so that you will be pleased with the life I live and the choices I make. Then I will know that you will be pleased with me and will provide me with the shelter of your love. I praise you and thank you. Amen.

May 7

A Psalm of David

"How great is your goodness, which you have stored up for those who fear you, which you bestow in the sight of men on those who take refuge in you. In the shelter of your presence you hide them from the intrigues of men, in your dwelling you keep them safe from accusing tongues."

Psalm 31:19-20

Dear Lord, I will fear you alone. You will keep me in the shelter of your presence. That is absolutely the safest place to be. That is where I want to be. In your dwelling, you will keep me safe. What a wonderful blanket of comfort and security you provide. I am so thankful. Amen.

May 8

A Psalm of David

"Be strong, and let your heart take courage, all you who wait for the Lord!"

Psalm 31:24

Dear Lord, my only hope is in you. Other people and things may disappoint me. You never will. If I trust in you, I can be strong. My heart will remain intact. You are my fortress. I am brave when I walk with you on the path you have chosen for me. I will always try to be patient and wait to see just what your plans are for me. I praise you and thank you for being the constant, steady force in my life. Amen.

Fear Not

May 9

A Psalm of David

"The king is not saved by his great army; a warrior is not delivered by his great strength. The war horse is a false hope for salvation, and by its great might it cannot rescue. Behold, the eye of the Lord is on those who fear him, on those who hope in his steadfast love, that he may deliver their soul from death and keep them alive in famine."

Psalm 33:16-19

Dear Lord, my strength comes from you. My safety comes from you. Today I saw on television an advertisement for a home security system. The speaker was appealing to everyone's desire to protect their loved ones and their possessions. There is only one who can offer that protection. That is the Lord. Security systems and police, firefighters and paramedics, can only help in the Lord's work. I am grateful to all the first responders. I do have locks on my doors. However, I am most grateful to you Lord, because you are the only force that I trust to keep me safe. Amen.

May 10

A Psalm of David

"I sought the Lord, and he answered me and delivered me from all my fears."

Psalm 34:4

Dear Lord, I will bless you at all times. I will praise you always by singing your name. Let me join in with others and lift up the name of the Lord. Help me be humble. Protect me from evil words and thoughts. Stay near me when I am troubled and brokenhearted. I thank you for being my salvation. Amen.

May 11

A Psalm of David

"Don't worry about the wicked or envy those who do wrong. For like grass, they soon fade away. Like spring flowers, they soon wither."

Psalm 37:1-2 NLT

Dear Lord, I praise you for trying to give me wisdom. I humbly hope I have learned something in my many years on earth. It does me no good to worry about the wrongdoings of others. It is hard enough to manage myself. I will try to live up to your hopes for me. I will pray for others. I will let you be the one to chastise or judge any other fellow man. I find myself wanting to fix people. Please help me remember that is your job. You can handle it. You are God. I thank you for all your great power. I can just be me. Amen.

May 12

A song of David

"Be still in the presence of the Lord, and wait patiently for him to act. Don't worry about evil people who prosper or fret about their wicked schemes."

Psalm 37:7 NLT

Dear Lord, I am so glad that is your job, not mine, to deal with punishing evildoers. I cannot be a judge because I do not know all the circumstances. You do. There will always be evil in this world. I will try to avoid evil thoughts and actions to the best of my ability, remembering that I am human and not perfect. But I need to concern myself with me and my relationship with you. Therefore I will continue to thank you for all my blessing, praise you always, and seek a closer relationship with you. Amen.

May 13

A Psalm of David

"Refrain from anger, and forsake wrath! Fret not yourself; it tends only to evil. For the evildoers shall be cut off, but those who wait for the Lord shall inherit the land."

Psalm 37:8-9

Dear Lord, I ask you to help me not to be angry or worry about people who commit crimes or profit from evil. If I fret about them, that will take up all my time. I would be unable to focus on anything else. I choose to focus on you. I want to think pure thoughts about all the good in this world and the next. Help me to focus on what is right and beautiful. I will try to keep my eyes on you, Lord. Amen.

May 14

A Psalm of David

"I kept quiet, not saying a word, not even about anything good! But my suffering only grew worse, and I was overcome with anxiety. The more I thought, the more troubled I became; I could not keep from asking: ..."

Psalm 39:2-3 GNT

Dear Lord, if I become troubled, my anxiety will grow, and more problems will develop. I may become discontent and forget about my gratuity. I may forget about all the wonderful things in this world and my life. That is why I need prayer instead of worry. I praise you for your scripture that continues to remind me of this. Thank you, Lord, for your word in my life. Amen.

Fear Not

May 15

A Psalm of the Sons of Korah

"God is our refuge and strength, a very present help in trouble. Therefore we will not fear though the earth gives way, though the mountains be moved into the heart of the sea, though its waters roar and foam, though the mountains tremble at its swelling."

Psalm 46:1-3 NIV

Dear Lord, no matter what happens, I will continue to praise you and know that you are God. Storms, volcanos, earthquakes may come, but you are still God. Wars will be fought, terrorists will attack, but you will still be God. I will find shelter in your presence. No matter what happens, you will be my refuge and my strength. I will give thanks to you no matter what happens. Amen.

May 16

The Lord is speaking in A Psalm of the Sons of Korah.

" 'Be still, and know that I am God. I will be exalted among the nations, I will be exalted in the earth!' The Lord of hosts is with us; the God of Jacob is our fortress."

Psalm 46:10-11

Dear Lord, Oh Lord, how I love to hear your voice! Your words are so very powerful. Lord, please help me to be still and know that you are God. That is the way to stop feeling worried or anxious. That is the way to stop being afraid. That is the way to find peace on this earth. Let me exalt you always. In you, I have a fortress. How can I even thank you enough for this? I praise your name. Amen.

May 17

A Psalm of the Sons of Korah

"Be not afraid when a man becomes rich, when the glory of his house increases."

Psalm 49:16

Dear Lord, I praise you for your greatness. I thank you for every day that I am alive. I see many people spend lots of energy worrying about their possessions. I sometimes worry about my bank account, despite the fact that you have told me not to. I have learned that all man's possessions amount to nothing. What matters is if he has God in his life. The more one devotes his life to you, the better that life will be. Rich or poor, it doesn't matter. You are what matters. Help me to always remember that as I go about my daily life. You are what is relevant. Amen.

May 18

A Psalm of David

"There they are, in great terror, where there is no terror! For God scatters the bones of him who encamps against you; you put them to shame, for God has rejected them."

Psalm 53:5

Dear Lord, I praise you. Your love endures forever. You, dear Lord, are my only strength. I can have no courage on my own. Sometimes I am afraid when there is no threat. Bad dreams can be like that. Walking in the dark can be like that. I will try to remember that you are beside me. You dwell in my heart. I will be safe. Amen.

May 19

A Psalm of David

"Listen, God, to my prayer! Don't reject my request. Please listen and help me. My thoughts are troubled, and I keep groaning because my loud enemies shout and attack. They treat me terribly and hold angry grudges."

Psalm 55:1-3 CEV

Dear Lord, today I will cast my cares upon you. I will trust only you. That is my safety. You are my security. Neither friends nor enemies may come against me. They may try their best to upset me. They may try to cause my mind to be troubled, but I will remember to be still and know that you are God. All will be as it should. Amen.

May 20

A Psalm of David

"Our Lord, we belong to you. We tell you what worries us, and you won't let us fall."

Psalm 55:22 CEV

Dear Lord, I thank you for allowing me to belong to you. That gives me security and the feeling of belonging to a large wonderful family. I can tell you anything. I know that when I have a problem I can give it to you. At that point, I do not need to be distressed about that problem any longer. You have it. No problem is too big for you. What a comfort! I praise you for your great power and overwhelming love. Amen.

May 21

David wrote this song when the Philistines seized him in Gath.

"When I am afraid, I put my trust in you. In God, whose word I praise, in God I trust; I shall not be afraid. What can flesh do to me?"

Psalm 56:3-4

Dear Lord, every day I praise you. I praise your holy word. I remember that it is your spiritual world in which I dwell. The earth is just my temporary home. Your love endures forever. I sing praises to your name and thank you for my blessings. Amen.

May 22

David wrote this song when the Philistines seized him in Gath.

"In God, whose word I praise, in the Lord, whose word I praise, in God I trust; I shall not be afraid. What can man do to me?"

Psalm 56:10-11

Dear Lord, thank you for the blessing of my life. I am grateful to you for every day I walk on this earth. Reading your word and studying the Bible has brought me great joy. Your love has made me brave and strong. You are with me and who can come against me? Amen.

May 23

This psalm of David is from when Saul sent men to watch David's house in order to kill him.

"O my Strength, I will watch for you, for you, O God, are my fortress. My God in his steadfast love will meet me; God will let me look in triumph on my enemies."

Psalm 59:9-10

Dear Lord, you alone are my strength. In this world today, I feel like I need a safe place. If things in this world get too crazy or feel too dangerous, I can remember that I have a fortress in the Lord. I can go to the shelter that you provide. Then I can feel safe. It seems like every week in the news I hear more stories that make this world feel so unsafe. But the media doesn't talk about that special place where God loves all his people. Amen.

May 24

This psalm of David is from when Saul sent men to watch David's house in order to kill him.

"O my Strength, I will sing praises to you, for you, O God, are my fortress, the God who shows me steadfast love."

Psalm 59:17

Dear Lord, when I am strong, I am able to feel braver. I feel more confident. I praise you because of how safe you make me feel. I like to imagine living with you in a big castle with strong, high rock walls that no enemy can penetrate. You can arm my body with that kind of a wall. That wall is your love, and you can prevent evil from entering. I just have to have faith and always believe. Oh Lord, give me the strength I need! Amen.

May 25

A Psalm of David

"He only is my rock and my salvation, my fortress;
I shall not be shaken. On God rests my salvation and
my glory; my mighty rock, my refuge is God. Trust
in him at all times, O people; pour out your heart
before him; God is a refuge for us."

Psalm 62:6-8

Dear Lord, you are my refuge. You are the only true refuge, so I trust mainly in you. Because of an increase in gun violence, mass shootings, and terrorist activity, the government has Homeland Security, Border Patrol, the FBI, the CIA, NSA, local law enforcement, airport security, metal detectors, no fly lists, but still, they cannot keep us safe. Only you can do that. That is why I praise you, I thank you, and I trust only you. Amen.

May 26

A Psalm of David

"Hear my voice, O God, in my complaint; preserve my life from dread of the enemy"

Psalm 64:1

Dear Lord, it is you alone that I sing praises to. Some days I feel like the world, and my country is broken. There is so much violence and fear. There has always been evil, but now the media is so filled with it. Only you can fix this. I know you have a plan and it will be carried out in your time. While I am here on earth, I pray you give me shelter and protection. You are my great comforter, and without you, I would be lost. I thank you for staying with me always. Amen.

May 27

A Psalm of Asaph

"My flesh and my heart may fail, but God is the strength of my heart and my portion forever."

Psalm 73:26

Dear Lord, this psalm that was written by your servant, Asaph, speaks to my heart. All the riches and the glories of this earth are nothing compared to you and your heavenly kingdom. Greed and envy are sins. I pray you will remove these sins from my heart. I want my heart to be full of my love for you. As I praise you and thank you for offering me life, let me remain humble and strive not for gains on this earth, but gains in your realm. Please hear my prayer and offer me your guidance. Amen.

May 28

A Psalm of Asaph

"He led them in safety, so that they were not afraid, but the sea overwhelmed their enemies."

Psalm 78:53

Dear Lord, I pray you will always lead me to safety. Help me to open my mind and my heart so when you guide me, I will follow. At times it is hard to hear your voice or know what path you want me to take. At times like that, remind me to pray and go to your word. I believe that if I sincerely ask for your guidance and I obey your commandments, my decisions will be accepted by you. Please, Lord, continue to safely lead me. Amen.

May 29

A Psalm of Asaph

"Blessed are those whose strength is in you, who have set their hearts on pilgrimage. As they pass through the Valley of Baca, they make it a place of springs; the autumn rains also cover it with pools. They go from strength to strength, till each appears before God in Zion."

Psalm 84:5-7 NIV

Dear Lord, you are my shield. As I trust in you, my faith increases and I get stronger. No matter where I am on this earth, in my heart, I will dwell in your house. My shelter is magnificent. You are with me, and the sun is shining. None can dim the light you shine on me. I praise you for the happiness you give me daily. I am grateful that I can be with you now and in eternity. Amen.

May 30

A prayer of David

"But you, O Lord, are a God, merciful and gracious, slow to anger and abounding in steadfast love and faithfulness. Turn to me and be gracious to me; give your strength to your servant, and save the son of your maidservant. Show me a sign of your favor, that those who hate me may see and be put to shame because you, Lord, have helped me and comforted me."

Psalm 86:15-17

Dear Lord, once again, your servant David has offered up a beautiful prayer. I can do no better. I hope no one hates me, but if they do, you can take care of that for me. I praise you. I thank you for your word. Amen.

Fear Not

May 31

A Psalm

"You will not fear the terror of the night, nor the arrow that flies by day, nor the pestilence that stalks in darkness, nor the destruction that wastes at noonday."

Psalm 91:5-6

Dear Lord, I praise you for knowing me and protecting me. Please command your angels to watch over me day and night. As I sleep, keep my dreams sweet. In you, Lord, I will always trust. You are my shelter. May I be as faithful to you in my trust, as you are to me in your everlasting love. Amen.

June 1

A Psalm

"When anxiety was great within me, your consolation brought joy to my soul."

Psalm 94:19 NIV

Dear Lord, today if I experience anxiety, I will give it to you. As often as I need to, I will ask you for help in removing the anxiety. You will comfort me. Then instead of feeling uncomfortable, I will feel great joy knowing that I belong to you and you are my shield and protector. This change in my feelings may not happen in one moment, but I will keep asking for your help. I praise you and thank you in advance for working this miracle in changing my attitude. Amen.

June 2

A Psalm

"Seek the Lord and his strength; seek his presence continually!"

Psalm 105:4

Dear Lord, your message today is especially helpful when I am faced with difficulties or hardships. The more I praise you, the closer I feel to your presence. That is important to me. I want to remember always to seek your presence. When things get tough, I will get stronger, but only if I exercise the muscles in my brain that think positive things about you all the time. Let me also exercise the gratuity muscle. I will say "Thank you, Thank you, Thank you, Lord," many times a day. And I will grow in your strength. Amen.

June 3

A Psalm

"He calmed the storm to a whisper and stilled the waves. What a blessing was that stillness as he brought them safely into harbor."

Psalm 107:29-30 NLV

Dear Lord, the ocean is your greatest art work. The ocean gives me my greatest inspiration. I can always find you on the beach. I hear your voice in the sound of the surf. There are many forces in this world that no man can control. They are very powerful. No matter how strong any man is, you are stronger. You are in charge of all natural forces. If I ever feel frightened by these forces, I need to remember that you alone are in charge. I will remain calm, knowing that when the time is right, you will calm the storm. You will lead me safely home. Amen.

Fear Not

A Psalm

"He is not afraid of bad news; his heart is firm, trusting in the Lord. His heart is steady; he will not be afraid, until he looks in triumph on his adversaries."

Psalm 112:7-8

Dear Lord, help me to be righteous. Help me to live the way you want me to live. I praise you for your perfect love. I thank you for all my blessings. I will fear only you, and know that you will allow me to grow in my knowledge of walking in your path, Lord, and doing your will. This is not easy, but you will be by my side. I will face whatever news might come my way, as long as you are with me. I especially will not be afraid of the bad news I see on television. Amen.

Fear Not

June 5

A Psalm

"I love the Lord because he hears my voice and my prayer for mercy. Because he bends down to listen, I will pray as long as I have breath! Death wrapped its ropes around me; the terrors of the grave overtook me. I saw only trouble and sorrow. Then I called on the name of the Lord: "Please, Lord, save me!" How kind the Lord is! How good he is! So merciful, this God of ours! The Lord protects those of childlike faith; I was facing death, and he saved me."

Psalms 116:1-6 NLT

Dear Lord, when I am afraid, all I have to do is call your name and you will give me rest. Amen.

June 6

A Psalm

"Let my soul be at rest again, for the Lord has been good to me."

Psalm 116:7 NLT

Dear Lord, if my mind is at peace, I will be well today. You have let me enjoy good health. When I did have a cancer diagnosis, you helped me to keep a positive attitude. I was able to handle the fear. When I wouldn't let fear have a grip on me, and I let you be one hundred percent in charge, my soul was at rest. I could heal. I praise you for that. I thank you many times for the peace and the healing. Dear Lord, please help me and others keep a calm attitude and a restful spirit, no matter what is happening in the material world. Amen.

June 7

A Psalm

"In my distress I prayed to the Lord, and the Lord answered me and set me free. The Lord is for me, so I will have no fear. What can mere people do to me?"

Psalm 118:5-6 NLT

Dear Lord, I am so in awe of you because your love endures forever. I thank you for my faith. My faith gives me a sense of inner strength and security. Today I will focus on what you, Lord, can do for me, not what people can do for me. I also will focus on what I can do to please you, Lord, not people. Today is the day you made, Lord. I will be glad in it and sing a song of praise to you. Amen.

June 8

A Psalm

"It is better to take refuge in the Lord than to trust in people. It is better to take refuge in the Lord than to trust in Princes".

Psalm 118:8-9 NLT

Dear Lord, I feel so protected because I know your love endures forever. You repeat that phrase many times in your scriptures. You alone are my refuge. Sometimes I feel very safe in my home, but then I realize that is only because you are there with me. We have been in that house through two tornados. Friends' homes have burned down. My home is still standing, but I know that if the building were destroyed tomorrow, I would still have a safe dwelling place with you. It is only you that makes me feel so safe. You have kept me safe so far. I trust you with my future. I praise you and thank you always. Amen.

June 9

A Psalm

"The Lord is my strength and my song; he has become my salvation."

Psalm 118:14

Dear Lord, once again I praise you for the strength you have given me. I have physical strength, and I can participate in many sports that I enjoy. But many are stronger and better athletes. Many people I know can lift more weight than I can. I work out, lift weights and try to be as physically strong as possible. But we all have different strengths. The strength you give me is courage, determination, faith and inner peace. I thank you for that. My faith is also a muscle that I must exercise, and with your help, my faith will continue to grow stronger. Amen.

June 10

A Psalm

"My soul melts away for sorrow; strengthen me according to your word!"

Psalm 119:28

Dear Lord, I thank you for continually giving me strength. Even in times of sorrow, you are there with comfort, and I can wake up each day and face it with courage. Some days can be harder than others. Those days it may be harder to find you or hear your voice, but you are there. Your love is steadfast, and joy will follow sorrow as sure a day follows night. So I will praise you in the dark of night and the brightness of day. You are the light. You are the joy I seek. Amen.

June 11

A Psalm

"Stress and strain have caught up with me, but your commandments are my joy!"

Psalm 119:143 CEB

Dear Lord, I am grateful to grow in my faith. I used to shudder at the very mention of the word "commandment." I had trouble with authority. I still do. I have trouble giving other people authority over my life. So it was hard to give you authority, Lord, but I hope I am doing better at submitting to your will and following your commandments. I don't like anyone telling me what to do, but you are not just anyone. You are the perfect God. I will follow your commands. They will give me joy. That is far better than stress and strain. I will not be afraid to submit to you. Then I need fear no other. Amen.

June 12

A song of ascents

"In my distress I called to the Lord, and he answered me."

Psalm 120:1

Dear Lord, I love peace. This psalm is about peace. To me love is peaceful. Today I saw some people grieving in the workplace. It seems one of their coworkers broke up with the girl he loved. He was distressed, so he went to her house, shot her, shot at her parents, left the house and got hit by a car and died. He thought he was in love with the girl, but that is not love. Love is peaceful. These events distressed me, so I turned to you. You answered me. That young man certainly felt tremendous distress. I don't know if he tried to turn to you or not. I am praying for all the people involved. I thank you for the comfort you will give to the grieving. I praise you for reminding me not to be afraid when horrible things happen near to me. You hold us all in your hands. Amen.

June 13

A Psalm of David

"On the day I called, you answered me; my strength of soul you increased."

Psalm 138:3

Dear Lord, I love to sing songs of praise to you. You go with me and protect me. You send bands of angels to surround me. They sing praises to you and turn all your enemies away. They will fight the evil forces for me and keep me safe. Their songs of joy lift my spirits. I am comforted when I need comforting. As the strength of my soul increases, my fear decreases. I am safe in your loving arms. I thank you, Lord. Amen.

June 14

A Psalm of David

"Search me, O God, and know my heart; test me and know my anxious thoughts. Point out anything in me that offends you, and lead me upon the path of everlasting life."

Psalm 139:23-24 NLT

Dear Lord, I praise you always for your excellent guidance. I know I need your constant supervision. I am like a lot of people. I want to do things on my own. Oh, but I can't. I want to be brave and strong. I want to quit worrying. I never want to feel anxious. I need your help. No one can do these things alone, especially me. Without you, I am a bundle of nerves and afraid of so many things. I also tend to think I am perfect sometimes. Show me all my sinful ways so I can repent, with your help. Again I cannot be forgiven without your help. I can't even ask for forgiveness without your help. Be my helper, Lord. Thank you. Amen.

June 15

A Psalm of David

"O Lord, my Lord, the strength of my salvation, you have covered my head in the day of battle."

Psalm 140:7

Dear Lord, my strength comes from you alone. You make it possible for me to be strong and live without fear. You have taught me to see only love and peace. If other forces exist, you will cover my heart, my head and my eyes with your righteousness. I will only see things which encourage me and bring me joy. Your ever enduring love builds me up. It gives me confidence. If a day of battle comes, I will hold my head high and march forward into victory. You and your band of angels are my warriors. Can anyone assemble a more powerful army? I praise you always. I give thanks for everything as you commanded. Amen.

June 16

A Psalm of David

"Blessed be the Lord, my rock, who trains my hands for war, and my fingers for battle; he is my steadfast love and my fortress, my stronghold and my deliverer, my shield and he in whom I take refuge, who subdues peoples under me."

Psalm 144:1-2

Dear Lord, you are my God, and you bring great joy to those who worship you. You are most blessed. I enjoy constantly praising you. As well as joy, you bring strength, confidence, courage, and comfort. You are my shield. You are the greatest refuge. You are in fact the only refuge. You bring your people joy, victory, and prosperity. We can walk through this world holding the mightiest sword and shield. Thank you, Lord. Amen.

June 17

A Proverb of Solomon, son of David, king of Israel

"Trust in the Lord with all your heart and lean not on your own understanding; in all your ways acknowledge him, and he will make your paths straight."

Proverbs 3:5-6 NIV

Dear Lord, this verse is one of my very favorites. This suggestion made by Solomon, the king known for his wisdom, is a guide to abundant, joyful living. Trusting in the Lord always and following His path, not my own, will keep me safe. I can bravely walk forward in my life, believing the choices I make are the correct ones, believing I have God's blessing. I will not fear. Amen.

June 18

A Proverb of Solomon

"If you lie down, you will not be afraid; when you lie down, your sleep will be sweet."

Proverbs 3:24

Dear Lord, please protect me day and night. Your love is always and forever. You watch over me day and night. For that, I praise you and thank you. I will rest peacefully and have sweet dreams knowing that I am safe in your loving arms. What a blessing! Amen.

June 19

A Proverb of Solomon

"Do not be afraid of sudden terror or of the ruin of the wicked, when it comes, for the Lord will be your confidence and will keep your foot from being caught."

Proverbs 3:25-26

Dear Lord, help me to trust in you with all my heart, and not try to trust in myself. Remind me to always to turn to you for all decisions. Keep me on the right path. I praise you in advance for leading me in the right direction. I thank you for your guidance. Help me to know your plan for me. Help me hear your voice. If I remain in your word, I need not fear threats of terrorism, crimes of this world or the trouble around me. Again I praise your name. Amen.

June 20

A Proverb of Solomon

"I have counsel and sound wisdom; I have insight; I have strength."

Proverbs 8:14

Dear Lord, I praise you and thank you in advance for any wisdom you may give me. Many times every day I have to make decisions. Some are small, and some are major. The only way I can make good decisions is to consult with you in prayer. I try to remember each morning to ask you to guide me all day. When I remember to pray about all decisions, they will all be the best decisions for me at that time. My insight and understanding come from you. It gives me strength and power. I will not be afraid to make a mistake. Amen.

Fear Not

June 21

A Proverb of Solomon

"Anxiety in a man's heart weighs him down, but a good word makes him glad."

Proverbs 12:25

Dear Lord, your proverbs are lessons to me about living a joy filled, abundant life. You are instructing me not to be anxious. That means; do not fear, do not worry, do not be afraid. I thank you, Lord, for your gentle instructions, your kind words, and your enduring love. I will do my best obey your words. I am therefore most grateful for the joy I experience by putting aside my anxious heart. This is only possible with your help. Amen.

Fear Not

A Proverb of Solomon

"One who is wise is cautious and turns away from evil, but a fool is reckless and careless."

Proverbs 14:16

Dear Lord, I praise you for your ever enduring love. I thank you for entering my life and staying with me. Help me remember that being fearless does not mean being reckless or stupid. My body is sacred, and you dwell in me. Therefore I will not do things on purpose which I know are unsafe. I can be sensible about risk taking. That is what wisdom is. That is the wisdom I pray you might grant me. I know you control everything, but I can help you to keep my loved ones and me healthy and safe. You gave me a brain, and I will try to use it. Keep me from evil as I try to be ever watchful to avoid it. Amen.

June 23

A Proverb

"A wise man is full of strength, and a man of knowledge enhances his might, for by wise guidance you can wage your war, and in abundance of counselors there is victory."

Proverbs 24:5-6

Dear Lord, today I have studied your word. Today I have read passages of the Bible, as well as passages by other great religious authors. If I face trials, your words, as well as your scholar' words can give me great strength. I praise you and thank you for not giving me any serious trials today, but I know they will return to my life at some time. May the wisdom offered me today by you and other wise counselors stay with me and be made available by you when needed. I will not be afraid of what the future may bring. I will not be afraid because I am trying to arm myself with wisdom and good counsel. Amen.

June 24

A Proverb

"If you faint in the day of adversity, your strength is small."

Proverbs 24:10

Dear Lord, without you, my strength is small. It is your spirit within me that gives me courage. It is the knowledge of you that gives me comfort. I have learned that when I face a terrifying situation, I automatically and instinctively turn to you. That is one of the reasons that I never lose faith. When I was in a car accident; when I was on a very scary ride at an amusement park; when I fell off of a horse and broke my arm; when I had a gun pointed at my head, at all those times, without thinking first I cried out to you for help. You comforted me. I will never forget those times. I will not faint. I will be strong. I will call out your name. I thank you, Lord, for always being close. You alone can save me. I praise your name. Amen.

June 25

A Proverb

"Don't let evil people worry you or make you jealous. They will soon be gone like the flame of a lamp that burns out."

Proverbs 24:19-20 CEV

Dear Lord, don't let me fret about what other people do. I have enough trouble keeping myself on the right path. I need to turn to you continually to live a joyous, abundant life filled with strength and faith. I am grateful that your love will be with me now and into eternity. I will try to love my neighbor as myself. I will ask you to remove all envy and jealousy and replace it with the kind of love you have shown me. I will try to be a light that will burn strong enough to show the way to any around who may be stumbling. I will ask for your help in all of this. I praise your power and love, Lord. Amen.

June 26

A Proverb of Solomon

"The wicked flee when no one pursues, but the righteous are bold as a lion."

Proverbs 28:1

Dear Lord, today I am not asking you to help me be brave. Instead, I am asking you to help me be righteous. As I have been reading these proverbs, I see how important it is to obey your laws. It is also important to obey the laws of the land. It is also important to be an ethical person and always try to do what is right, even when no one is watching because you are always watching. If I can be blessed with doing what is right, I do not need to fear the police, the lawyers, the Internal Revenue Service, or bill collectors. The lawbreakers must live in constant fear of being caught. I am at peace. If I can succeed at being righteous, you will make me bold. Amen.

June 27

A Proverb

"The fear of man lays a snare, but whoever trusts in the Lord is safe"

Proverbs 29:25

Dear Lord, I will fear only you. Man cannot hurt me. Let your wisdom keep me from fools. Let me praise you. I give you thanks for all my blessings. I ask you for wisdom, knowledge, and understanding, but I know these gifts come only from you. Please help me be humble, generous and walk in your path. I want to remember that with wisdom comes the knowledge that there are many things I cannot know or understand. Only you know the "why" of why certain things happen. Only you can unravel the mysteries of creation and life forces. Only you know what is to come. Amen.

June 28

This verse is from the oft quoted proverb that discusses a wife of noble character.

"She has no fear of winter for her household, for everyone has warm clothes."

Proverbs 31:21 NLT

Dear Lord, I praise you and thank you for all my blessings. When I have enough food, a warm house, and comfortable clothes it is much easier to be grateful to you and thank you for my blessings. Who can live up to the description of the noble woman described in this proverb? But I try to be my best. I can be sensible and use my resources to have a secure home, warm, sensible clothing and healthy food. All the other material things of this world that I may want are not necessary. You will provide for my needs, not my wants. Help me to live a modest, humble life. Keep me wrapped in the warmth of your love. Let my life be productive and pleasing to you. Amen.

June 29

This verse is from the oft quoted proverb that discusses a wife of noble character.

"She is clothed with strength and dignity, and she laughs without fear of the future."

Proverbs 31:25 NLT

Dear Lord, I love this verse. Please, Lord, give me the gift of being able to laugh without fear of the future. I believe one of the greatest gifts you have given me is my sense of humor. I pray you give that gift generously to lots of people. The world is a better place when we laugh. I want to do what is necessary, get the job done, but have fun while I do it. I don't think you put me on earth to be somber and serious. I try to be sensible with my resources and not be reckless, but I will have fun and laugh a lot and help me, Lord, to not worry about tomorrow. You have it taken care of. Amen.

June 30

This is David questioning the meaning of life.

"So what do people get in this life for all their hard work and anxiety? Their days of labor are filled with pain and grief; even at night their minds cannot rest. It is all meaningless."

Ecclesiastes 2:22-23

Dear Lord, I am grateful to you even when life seems very difficult. I believe hard work has its own merit, but I don't believe I should suffer from an anxious heart. I have been praying for the end to fear, worry, and anxiety. To me, those emotions can be meaningless. What good can come from worry and anxiety? I pray you will bless me with sound sleep and pleasant dreams. I know David was searching for the meaning of existence in this book of the Bible. I know that there is no meaning without you. You are the meaning of life. Amen.

July 1

David writes about how meaningless riches are.

"God gives some people the ability to enjoy the wealth and property he gives them, as well as the ability to accept their state in life and enjoy their work. They do not worry about how short life is, because God keeps them busy with what they love to do."

Ecclesiastes 5:19-20 NCV

Dear Lord, I delight in your blessings and thank you for meeting all my needs today. I thank you for the active, productive life I am able to lead. You have given me a good attitude about life. I could see people who have more riches than I do and be envious, but with your help, I am not doing that. I try with your help to not worry about my age or how short my days left on earth may be. I will live every day I have left on earth to the fullest. I will try to be as happy as I can. I feel secure in your love now and into eternity. Amen.

July 2

David writes about true wisdom, the fear of God.

"If you worry about the weather and don't plant seeds, you won't harvest a crop."

Ecclesiastes 11:4 CEV

Dear Lord, I praise you for being with me. I praise you in advance for rescuing me from worry. Help me make decisions and live my life based on a deep trust in your love. I can't worry about what might happen because I don't know and I can't control it. That is your job. Let me get out of your way and let you take care of me as you always do. I will plant seeds. Only you can make them grow. Help me to live a joyous, prosperous life filled with love for you. Amen.

July 3

David writes about true wisdom, the fear of God.

"So then, banish anxiety from your heart and cast off troubles of your body, for youth and vigor are meaningless."

Ecclesiastes 11:10 NIV

Dear Lord, I praise you for your word and the wisdom it imparts. It can be so simple. Seek only you, seek peace, and find it. The only thing in life that has meaning is you. I am working to banish anxiety from my heart. I will fill my heart with your holy spirit, so overflowing, that there will be room for nothing but peaceful, loving thoughts. I will do this today because life is short. Our time on earth is fleeting. Youth has already left me but let me be an example to the young that a wonderful life exists when youth passes. We should all focus on you, Lord and strive to nourish our souls, not our vanity. Help me and my acquaintances remember this. I thank you for my peace, Lord. Amen.

July 4

David is speaking about remembering God, the Creator, before he is overtaken by old age.

"Remember him before you become fearful of falling and worry about danger in the streets, before your hair turns white like an almond tree in bloom, and you drag along without energy like a dying grasshopper, and the caperberry no longer inspires sexual desire. Remember him before you near the grave, your everlasting home, when the mourners will weep at your funeral".

Ecclesiastes 12:5 NLT

Dear Lord, help me always to remember you, the creator. Today is a holiday. There will be lots of fireworks, noise, good food and celebration. Let me enjoy the festivities while I am able, always keeping you in mind. I will celebrate the blessings of my country and thank you for an abundant life. You created it all. Amen.

July 5

The Lord is speaking to Isaiah.

"Be careful, be quiet, do not fear, and do not let your heart be faint because of these two smoldering stumps of firebrands, at the fierce anger of Rezin and Syria and the son of Remaliah."

Isaiah 7:4

Dear Lord, I praise you. I praise your name. I thank you for the spirit of peace. I will try with your help to be prudent. I will not be afraid. Let my heart be filled with a spirit of strength. Only then with your help can I stand up against anyone who tries to hurt me. Thank you in advance, Lord, for you constant protection. Amen

Fear Not

July 6

The Lord is speaking to Isaiah.

"Do not call conspiracy all that this people calls conspiracy, and do not fear what they fear, nor be in dread. But the Lord of hosts, him you shall honor as holy. Let him be your fear, and let him be your dread ..."

Isaiah 8:12-13

Dear Lord, in today's commotion, please help me to be still. Grant me peace. I praise you for your comfort. I praise you for your perfect plan. I thank you for the eyes to see the world as it is, your creation. Remind me that worrying is a sin. It is wrong. I will fear nothing in this world. I will fear only you. Peace will be with me. Of that, you have assured me. Again, God, I thank you. Amen.

July 7

The Lord is speaking to Isaiah.

"Therefore thus says the Lord God of hosts: "O my people, who dwell in Zion, be not afraid of the Assyrians when they strike with the rod and lift up their staff against you as the Egyptians did ..."

Isaiah 10:24

Dear Lord, I praise you for your power. I thank you for your kindness. I know you will protect me from any evil forces. Please keep me safe, Oh Lord. Amen.

Fear Not

July 8

Isaiah tells how the people of Israel will sing praise to the Lord.

"Behold, God is my salvation; I will trust, and will not be afraid; for the Lord God is my strength and my song, and he has become my salvation."

Isaiah 12:2

Dear Lord, thank you for always being there for me, even on those days when I'm not there for you. There are days that I forget you. There are times when I act poorly and do not honor you. At times I may turn away from you. You may be angry, but you are still there to comfort me. I trust you completely, so I never need to be afraid. When I do fear, you remind me that you are my strength. I praise you. Amen.

July 9

This is a prophesy of Isaiah concerning Damascus.

"The cities of Aroer are deserted; they will be for flocks, which will lie down, and none will make them afraid."

Isaiah 17:2

Dear Lord, in your wisdom you sometimes wreak havoc. I don't always understand. That is ok. But the brave go on. They get up and keep going. They fight back. They rebuild. In the last few decades of my life, I have survived hurricanes and tornadoes close up and personal. I have watched dozens of attacks by terrorists, including the attacks of 9/11. And I have seen the amazing recoveries. I will march into the future with faith. I will be fearless. I trust in you. Amen.

July 10

Isaiah praises the Lord

"For you have been a stronghold to the poor, a stronghold to the needy in his distress, a shelter from the storm and a shade from the heat; for the breath of the ruthless is like a storm against a wall,"

Isaiah 25:4

Dear Lord, I am so grateful to you. You are always with me. You are my shelter. I know you will be with me in times of trouble. As the storms approach, I ask you to hold my hand. If needed, wrap your loving arms around me. Bring relief to all the suffering people I see. Let me help you in bringing comfort to the needy if I am able. Give me the tools and the power to honor you by helping your children. I praise you and thank you, Lord, for the strong shelter you provide. Amen.

July 11

Isaiah praises the Lord.

"Trust in the Lord God always, for in the Lord Jehovah is your everlasting strength."

Isaiah 26:4 TLB

Dear Lord, today I heard a missionary say, "I am immortal until the Lord is finished using me." Lord, I hope I can be of service to you. You are my strength. With you by my side, I am fearless. I pray today that the strength you have been giving me is everlasting. I will be strong until the day you call me to be with you. I am grateful that you have found places in your kingdom to use me. Please allow me to continue to serve. Every day I turn to you for strength to keep on going. Let's get the everlasting job done together. There are always needs. I am proud to serve you and my fellow man. Amen.

July 12

Through Isaiah, the Lord is speaking to the people of Israel.

"For thus said the Lord God, the Holy One of Israel, 'In returning and rest you shall be saved; in quietness and in trust shall be your strength.'"

Isaiah 30:15

Dear Lord, I need your strength today. This morning I felt tired and didn't want to get out of bed. Outside it was dreary, wet and windy. I had to pray to you just to get going. My mind feels restless. I am constantly seeking possessions and pleasure. Yet I need nothing. This verse is a wonderful reminder to me to be still. I told myself to quit thinking about what I wanted, and what to do next, but now you are speaking to me. I will try very hard to listen. I know that when you speak to me, you are serious and you mean it. In quietness and rest I will find my strength. Thank you Lord. Amen.

July 13

The Lord is speaking through Isaiah, warning the people to trust in him, not Egypt.

"For thus the Lord said to me, 'As a lion or a young lion growls over his prey, and when a band of shepherds is called out against him he is not terrified by their shouting or daunted at their noise, so the Lord of hosts will come down to fight on Mount Zion and on its hill. Like birds hovering, so the Lord of hosts will protect Jerusalem; he will protect and deliver it; he will spare and rescue it.'"

Isaiah 31:4-5

Dear Lord, I praise you for your power. At this time I feel there may be forces trying to harm our country. I pray that all our citizens, politicians, military and government officials can have hearts turned toward you Lord. Then you will guard our nation like a fierce lion. I pray we turn toward you and honor you. Lord, send your angels and disciples to guard our nation. I thank you. Amen.

July 14

Isaiah speaks to the women of Jerusalem.

"God's people will be free from worries, and their homes peaceful and safe."

Isaiah 32:18 GNT

Dear Lord, today I praise you and thank you for my home in which I feel safe and at peace. I do not have a perfect home. All my relationships are not perfect. But your love is perfect. I am one with your holy presence. You are in my home. You rule my life. Being at one with the Lord frees me from all my worries. All problems I think I have are simply in my mind. I will quiet my mind and dwell quietly at peace in my home. I thank you for this privilege. I am graced with this privilege by resting in my faith and trust in you. Amen.

July 15

Isaiah describes the joy of the redeemed as is told in scripture.

"Strengthen the weak hands, and make firm the feeble knees. Say to those who have an anxious heart, 'Be strong; fear not! Behold, your God will come with vengeance, with the recompense of God. He will come and save you.'"

Isaiah 35:3-4

Dear Lord, again you have commanded me to be strong. You have commanded me to fear not. After studying your word, I feel stronger and braver than yesterday or the day before. I am growing in your word. My body and my soul feel strengthened by your love and power. Lord, I humbly thank you and with praise I ask you to let me continue to grow in faith and trust every day. Amen.

July 16

The Lord is speaking through the prophet Isaiah about the deliverance of Jerusalem.

"When the servants of King Hezekiah came to Isaiah, Isaiah said to them, 'Say to your master, 'Thus says the Lord: Do not be afraid because of the words that you have heard, with which the young men of the king of Assyria have reviled me ...','"

Isaiah 37:5-6

Dear Lord, I praise your glory. I thank you for my courage. Do not let words hurt me. Do not let other's words cause me to worry. I will stay courageous and not let others sway my trust in you. You are my rock. When people come against me, it is their problem, not mine. Amen.

July 17

Isaiah prophesies about God's comfort for his people.

"Go on up to a high mountain, O Zion, herald of good news; lift up your voice with strength, O Jerusalem, herald of good news; lift it up, fear not; say to the cities of Judah, 'Behold your God!'"

Isaiah 40:9

Dear Lord, grant me courage. When you are with me, I will have no fear. Let me walk and talk with strength. I praise you. Let your power come through me and pass to others. I thank you Lord for all my blessings. Amen.

July 18

Isaiah prophesies about God's comfort for his people.

"Have you not known? Have you not heard? The Lord is the everlasting God, the Creator of the ends of the earth. He does not faint or grow weary; his understanding is unsearchable."

Isaiah 40:28

Dear Lord, I praise you for so many things. I am thinking today about how you never go to sleep. You take no vacations. You are always there, you never get tired and you are never afraid or weak. Your strength is infinite. Your strength has no limits. Thankfully you are on my team. That puts me in a good position. I thank you for always being on my side. Please stay with me day and night, in all my endeavors. I will not fear. I have you as my leader and my partner. Amen.

July 19

Isaiah prophesies about God's comfort for his people.

"He gives power to the faint, and to him who has no might he increases strength."

Isaiah 40:29

Dear Lord, I am slowly learning to seek you any time I feel like I need more strength or courage. A short simple prayer can give great strength to my soul. A prayer can even increase my physical strength. When I exert myself through hard work or exercise, I can turn to you and offer a short prayer. It can be as invigorating as deep breathing to increase my oxygen supply or drinking a sports drink for quick energy. Likewise, if something frightens me, I can turn to you in prayer and my fears will be calmed. You really are a marvelous God. I am so thankful to have you so close. Amen.

July 20

Isaiah prophesies about God's comfort for his people.

"Even youths shall faint and be weary, and young men shall fall exhausted; but they who wait for the Lord shall renew their strength; they shall mount up with wings like eagles; they shall run and not be weary; they shall walk and not faint."

Isaiah 40:30-31

Dear Lord, you alone give me strength and courage in all situations. In this world there may come a situation where most people could not manage. But I will wait upon the Lord. With your help, Lord, I will be strong and face those situations. I will not be weak. I will not go into shock or faint. I will stay focused on you, Lord. You will walk me through any trial. That is why I stay with you. I thank you, Lord. I praise you, Lord. Amen.

July 21

God speaks through Isaiah offering promises of divine deliverance.

"... Everyone helps his neighbor and says to his brother, 'Be strong!'"

Isaiah 41:6

Dear Lord, I am seeking you today. I know you have things you want from me. Sometimes your people forget to turn to you for the strength and courage they need. I am asking you to help me with this task of reminding them to always turn to you for their needs. I know that sometimes you let us mortals help our brothers when in need. You are there, but you call on us to work with you at times. Help me with this task. Give me the words and the personality that allows me to share your word with my fellow man when they are weak or afraid. I humbly accept this job I feel you have given me. I praise you and thank you. Amen.

Fear Not

July 22

God speaks through Isaiah offering promises of divine deliverance.

"... fear not, for I am with you; be not dismayed, for I am your God; I will strengthen you, I will help you, I will uphold you with my righteous right hand ..."

Isaiah 41:10

Dear Lord, I praise you. Your companionship is so strong, so powerful. The more I walk with you, the closer you become. When you are with me, my strength is renewed. I am brave. I feel like I can soar with the eagles, run and not be weary, walk and not be faint. These are your words, Lord. These words are in your scriptures. The more I study, the more powerful I become, with you holding me with your right hand. I thank you Lord, for always staying by my side, even though I may sometimes wander away from you. Please keep me close and watch over me and my family. Amen.

July 23

God speaks through Isaiah offering promises of divine deliverance.

"For I, the Lord your God, hold your right hand; it is I who say to you, 'Fear not, I am the one who helps you.'"

Isaiah 41:13

Dear Lord, you are the great helper. I am safe because my helper is the greatest one. You are so great that we humans can hardly understand. Please stay close and guide me as I praise you. I thank you Lord for your blessings. Amen.

July 24

God speaks through Isaiah offering promises of divine deliverance.

"'Fear not, you worm Jacob, you men of Israel! I am the one who helps you,' declares the Lord; your Redeemer is the Holy One of Israel."

Isaiah 41:14

Dear Lord, I praise your great power. Without you I am nothing. I can do nothing. With you as my helper, I am strong, brave and my life has meaning. You are everything to me, God. I love you. I thank you for standing by me. Amen.

Fear Not

July 25

God speaks through Isaiah offering promises of divine deliverance.

"But now thus says the Lord, he who created you, O Jacob, he who formed you, O Israel: 'Fear not, for I have redeemed you; I have called you by name, you are mine ...'"

Isaiah 43:1

Dear Lord, I praise you and I am grateful to be your child. You know my name. I belong to you. You call my name when I am troubled. You are faithful to me. You protect me when hard times come to our nation. You will bring us through if we will only turn to you. Please be with us Lord. Amen.

July 26

God speaks through Isaiah offering promises of divine deliverance.

"Fear not, for I am with you; I will bring your offspring from the east, and from the west I will gather you."

Isaiah 43:5

Dear Lord, you are the one and only God, the all-powerful one. None come before or after you. You have created all things. Without you I am nothing. Be with me and give me strength. Any courage I may have comes from you. Allow me at times to be strong and silent; to be still; to be at peace. Amen.

July 27

God speaks through Isaiah offering promises of divine deliverance.

"Thus says the Lord who made you, who formed you from the womb and will help you: Fear not, O Jacob my servant, Jeshurun whom I have chosen."

Isaiah 44:2

Dear Lord, I praise you. I know you are totally in charge of everything. You control my life. You control all of the events of the world. My job is to love you, praise you and give thanks. All will be as it should. Amen.

Fear Not

July 28

God speaks through Isaiah offering promises of divine deliverance.

"... Fear not, nor be afraid; have I not told you from of old and declared it? 1 And you are my witnesses! Is there a God besides me? There is no Rock; I know not any."

Isaiah 44:8

Dear Lord, you alone are God, the only solid foundation that exists. When I feel fear, I need to wrap myself in your loving arms, praise you, give thanks and know that you alone are my God. Amen.

July 29

The Lord is speaking to prophet Isaiah.

"... Listen to me, you who know righteousness, the people in whose heart is my law; fear not the reproach of man, nor be dismayed at their revilings ..."

Isaiah 51:7

Dear Lord, I look to you who created me and all my ancestors. I look to the heavens. I look to the earth. Only my salvation will last forever. The rest will die. Righteousness will prevail. Man is not a threat. You, Lord, are the great protector. I thank you for keeping me in the safety of the shadow of your right hand. I praise you, Lord. Amen.

July 30

Isaiah the prophet responds to God after God speaks about the everlasting salvation of Zion.

"Awake, awake, put on strength, O arm of the Lord; awake, as in days of old, the generations of long ago. Was it not you who cut Rahab in pieces, who pierced the dragon?"

Isaiah 51:9

Dear Lord, your servant Isaiah knew first hand of your great power. So do I. I am not a prophet, but I feel your presence. I know you are the creator. You are the one with all the strength. Let the strength of your arms shelter me and give strength to my humble body. Make me strong and brave in your image. Turn away fear, weakness and disease. Put me in your loving embrace and let no mortal forces enter my place of safety. I will trust in you until eternal salvation. Amen.

July 31

The Lord is speaking to prophet Isaiah.

"I, I am he who comforts you; who are you that you are afraid of man who dies, of the son of man who is made like grass, and have forgotten the Lord, your Maker, who stretched out the heavens and laid the foundations of the earth, and you fear continually all the day because of the wrath of the oppressor, when he sets himself to destroy? And where is the wrath of the oppressor?..."

Isaiah 51:12-13

Dear Lord, today I come to you with humility in my heart. I fall short so often by not trusting you completely. I have been learning through this study of fear that I must only trust you. I must trust you completely and all the time. I must have unshakable faith in heaven and everlasting life. Dear Lord, please help me to be stronger in my faith and trust as I turn to you and surrender. Amen.

August 1

God is speaking through prophet Isaiah about the future glory of Zion.

"Fear not, for you will not be ashamed; be not confounded, for you will not be disgraced; for you will forget the shame of your youth, and the reproach of your widowhood you will remember no more ..."

Isaiah 54:4

Dear Lord, great is your compassion and your forgiveness. Old guilt is gone. You forgive me so I must forgive myself. I have not always felt you beside me, but you were near, and now you have made yourself known to me. I thank you for that. I know you love me and are devoted to me. Today I will devote my thoughts to you. Amen.

August 2

God is speaking through prophet Isaiah about the future glory of Zion.

"... In righteousness you shall be established; you shall be far from oppression, for you shall not fear; and from terror, for it shall not come near you ..."

Isaiah 54:14

Dear Lord, I know your promises to your people. Those are the people who love and worship you. I will stay with you. Therefore, the dangers of the world will not come near me. Please continue to protect my family in these trying times. I praise your holy name. I thank you for being on my side. Amen.

August 3

God is speaking through prophet Isaiah to establish the final kingdom. He is now addressing those who have not been faithful to him. I am including a note here that I recommend reading Isaiah 55. It is not on the topic of fear, but so beautiful.

"Whom did you dread and fear, so that you lied, and did not remember me, did not lay it to heart? Have I not held my peace, even for a long time, and you do not fear me?"

Isaiah 57:4

Dear Lord, I understand that you want me to fear only you. That means no idols. I will not worship my job, my money or even my family. I will not worry about finances or my family's health. I will exercise and enjoy sports, but take care not to put too much importance on those things. I praise you and thank you for any wisdom you give me that may help me to walk in peace. Amen.

August 4

God is speaking to Jeremiah.

"... Do not be afraid of them, for I am with you to deliver you, declares the Lord."

Jeremiah 1:8

Dear Lord, I praise you. I thank you for being with me. With you by my side, I am safe. When I feel insecure, please speak to me and remind me that you are there. I see your glory all around me. In that I rejoice. Amen.

August 5

The Lord is speaking to the people of Israel, through Jeremiah, about idolatry.

"This is what the Lord says: "Do not learn the ways of the nations or be terrified by signs in the sky, though the nations are terrified by them ..."

Jeremiah 10:2 NIV

Dear Lord, today I would like to truly thank you for the life I have and everything you have blessed me with. My greatest blessing is my faith in you. I will go about my life today without fear or worry. I am at peace knowing that you are in control. I will not look for signs of things to come. The future will be here and you will still be in control. If there is a warning or direction that you want me to go in, I will know. You will make your voice clear to me. I just need to listen. Amen.

August 6

The Lord is speaking to the people of Israel, through Jeremiah, about idolatry.

"... Their idols are like scarecrows in a cucumber field, and they cannot speak; they have to be carried, for they cannot walk. Do not be afraid of them, for they cannot do evil, neither is it in them to do good."

Jeremiah 10:5

Dear Lord, I praise you for all you have created. I thank you for the peace and beauty in my life. In this country today there are many false idols. They cannot harm me. You are the only one with power over me. Stay by my side and keep me on your path. Amen.

August 7

Jeremiah is speaking about idolatry.

"O Lord, my strength and my fortress, my refuge in time of distress, to you the nations will come from the ends of the earth and say, 'Our fathers possessed nothing but false gods, worthless idols that did them no good. Do men make their own gods? Yes, but they are not gods!'"

Jeremiah 16:19-20 NIV

Dear Lord, it is so wonderful to have you as my strength and my fortress. You have built walls of protection around me. You have given me a place to hide when trouble comes. Religious laws can get complicated, but to me this is simple. I will follow you, the one true God, and you will keep my path straight. I will put you first in my life. You will be my great leader, protector, comforter, and friend. I thank you for being with me. Amen.

August 8

This is what the Lord says to Jeremiah describing a man who fears God.

"... Blessed is the man who trusts in the Lord, whose trust is the Lord. He is like a tree planted by water, that sends out its roots by the stream, and does not fear when heat comes, for its leaves remain green, and is not anxious in the year of drought, for it does not cease to bear fruit."

Jeremiah 17:7-8

Dear Lord, I praise you. I thank you. You have given me roots. After years of wandering, you have helped me find a safe place to live and worship. I am constantly rooted in your love. I am physically and spiritually rooted in your community. I am watered by your words. All this helps me feel safe and secure at all times. I can stand firm through storms. Please stay by my side, Lord, and keep me grounded. Amen.

Fear Not

August 9

Jeremiah is speaking to God.

"Be not a terror to me; you are my refuge in the day of disaster."

Jeremiah 17:17

Dear Lord, this world seems like it's in a mess right now. Many predict disaster is coming. Let me not be fearful of you because I am trying to do your will. Let me not be fearful of the world, because you are my protector. I praise you for the comfort you give. I thank you for your protection and letting me know that you are in control. Amen.

August 10

The Lord is speaking through Jeremiah to shepherds who care for his people.

"Therefore thus says the Lord, the God of Israel, concerning the shepherds who care for my people: 'You have scattered my flock and have driven them away, and you have not attended to them. Behold, I will attend to you for your evil deeds, declares the Lord. Then I will gather the remnant of my flock out of all the countries where I have driven them, and I will bring them back to their fold, and they shall be fruitful and multiply. I will set shepherds over them who will care for them, and they shall fear no more, nor be dismayed, neither shall any be missing, declares the Lord...'"

Jeremiah 23:2-4

Dear Lord, you are the shepherd and I am the lamb. Please watch over me. You will not allow me to be lost. This is a big crazy world. Help me find my place. I praise you for watching over me and your flock. Amen

Fear Not

August 11

The Lord is speaking through Jeremiah.

"Then fear not, O Jacob my servant, declares the Lord, nor be dismayed, O Israel; for behold, I will save you from far away, and your offspring from the land of their captivity. Jacob shall return and have quiet and ease, and none shall make him afraid ..."

Jeremiah 30:10

Dear Lord, I praise you. I thank you for all my blessings. I appreciate the land of freedom I live in. I pray that all your lost children are returned home. There are whole countries today who are cast out. Let those people find lands of peace. Be with all who are lost. Remove the fear and give them peace. Keep us safe and help us feel secure. You are the great comforter. Again I praise your name. You are in charge. Amen.

August 12

The Lord is speaking to Jeremiah while he is held captive.

"... But I will deliver you on that day, declares the Lord, and you shall not be given into the hand of the men of whom you are afraid. For I will surely save you, and you shall not fall by the sword, but you shall have your life as a prize of war, because you have put your trust in me, declares the Lord."

Jeremiah 39:17-18

Dear Lord, just as you have rescued Jeremiah, I trust you to rescue me from any strongholds that may be affecting me. If I have bad habits, unhealthy thoughts or attitudes, you can rescue me. Lord, I submit to you and ask you to show me my faults, help me to do better, and save me from any evil that might come my way. Help me to totally trust you and increase my faith. Amen.

August 13

Jeremiah continues to prophesy.

"Gedaliah the son of Ahikam, son of Shaphan, swore to them and their men, saying, 'Do not be afraid to serve the Chaldeans. Dwell in the land and serve the king of Babylon, and it shall be well with you...'"

Jeremiah 40:9

Dear Lord, I give praise to you. Your love endures forever. Whatever the situation with our government and our leaders, I will not be afraid. You are in control. I will try my best to serve you. You are always with me. I thank you for your steadfast love. I know it is everlasting. Amen.

August 14

Jeremiah is reporting what God said in response to Johanan's request. Johanan agreed to have his people listen and obey God's word.

"Do not fear the king of Babylon, of whom you are afraid. Do not fear him, declares the Lord, for I am with you, to save you and to deliver you from his hand."

Jeremiah 42:11

Dear Lord, you are the king and the leader. I will fear no other. I will always praise you and thank you for your constant love. I will do my best to follow your word and do your will. Amen.

Fear Not

August 15

The Lord is speaking through Jeremiah.

"But fear not, O Jacob my servant, nor be dismayed, O Israel, for behold, I will save you from far away, and your offspring from the land of their captivity. Jacob shall return and have quiet and ease, and none shall make him afraid."

Jeremiah 46:27

Dear Lord, as always I praise you and give you thanks. You give me peace. Please pass this blessing on to my children and their children. Let our lives be filled with quiet and ease. Give us rest when needed. With you by our side, everything will be alright. We love you as you love us. Amen.

August 16

The Lord is speaking through Jeremiah.

"Fear not, O Jacob my servant, declares the Lord, for I am with you. I will make a full end of all the nations to which I have driven you, but of you I will not make a full end. I will discipline you in just measure, and I will by no means leave you unpunished."

Jeremiah 46:28

Dear Lord, I know that you are always with me. For that I am grateful. I praise you. You are so wonderful. You will help me to do the right thing. I know that if I do what is not right by you, there will be consequences. You are my partner forever. Things may not always turn out the way I want, but my beloved Lord will be with me. What more could I want? Amen.

Fear Not

August 17

This is what the Lord says to Jeremiah.

"Let not your heart faint, and be not fearful at the report heard in the land, when a report comes in one year and afterward a report in another year, and violence is in the land, and ruler is against ruler."

Jeremiah 51:46

Dear Lord, I will be very careful not to listen to rumors and false reports about things happening in this world today. The media is always trying to alarm people with reports of terrorism, foreign wars, domestic protests, and violence in our streets, nuclear threats and bad weather. Some of the reports are true. But the media focuses so much on all the terrible things of this world. Then the common people hear the stories, and often misinterpret them. I will trust in you and not be troubled over news reports or talk of people I come in contact with daily. I will focus on you and your everlasting love. Amen.

August 18

Jeremiah now mourns for Jerusalem after its destruction.

"You came near when I called on you; you said, 'Do not fear!'"

Lamentations 3:57

Dear Lord, you have told great men in the past, "Do not fear." You say it many times. Today our country seems to be in peril. You continue to tell me, "Do not fear." Lord, I praise your words. I need strength from you to believe those words and to know, deep in my soul, that they are true. How many times do I need to be told? Like a child who continues to disobey their parents, I continue to worry and fret. Forgive me, Lord. Know that I love you. I do know that your love endures forever. What more do I need to know? I thank you, Lord. I praise you. I will keep you by my side. Amen.

Fear Not

August 19

God is speaking through his prophet Ezekiel to the people of Israel.

"And you, son of man, be not afraid of them, nor be afraid of their words, though briers and thorns are with you and you sit on scorpions. Be not afraid of their words, nor be dismayed at their looks, for they are a rebellious house."

Ezekiel 2:6

Dear Lord, you are whom I praise. You are whom I put before all others. I thank you for your protection. People may say or do hurtful things, but your opinion is what is important to me. Hard times may come, trouble may come, but you will be there. Let them bully. Let them gossip. I have the Lord with me, holding me in his arms, comforting me. Humans and monsters cannot scare me. I fear only you, Lord. Please keep me in your loving care. I praise you. Amen.

August 20

The Lord is speaking to Ezekiel.

"... Like emery harder than flint have I made your forehead. Fear them not, nor be dismayed at their looks, for they are a rebellious house."

Ezekiel 3:9

Dear Lord, I praise you for your constant love. I thank you for my life. I thank you for my faith. Please remind me that when people say negative things about me or to me, or give me dirty looks, they are just being rebellious. They are the ones with the problem. Help the others in my family, in my workplace, or in my social circles to find your love and peace. Soften all our hearts. I praise you Lord. I thank you for the peace you bring. Amen.

August 21

Ezekiel is reporting what the Lord has said to him.

"So will I satisfy my wrath on you, and my jealousy shall depart from you. I will be calm and will no more be angry."

Ezekiel 16:42

Dear Lord, I know that anger is an emotion we all experience at times. But anger is a negative emotion that I can learn to control. You are my God and you are a loving God. If I want to be your child, I must have loving thoughts. I can put away any angry thoughts that I may have. Instead, I can look on any situation with your loving heart and eyes. With your help, I will see any disturbing situation with a new perspective. Only when I do this, will I be calm and at peace. I thank you for your word which gives me peace. I will remain calm even if someone or something tries to anger me. I praise the calm peace that comes from you, Lord. Amen.

August 22

Ezekiel is reporting what the Lord has said to him.

"They shall no more be a prey to the nations, nor shall the beasts of the land devour them. They shall dwell securely, and none shall make them afraid."

Ezekiel 34:28

Dear Lord, I praise you. I know that you are the Lord. You are my security. I dwell in your house. Peace is there. In this uncertain world, I am safe. For this, Lord, I thank you. Amen.

August 23

The Lord is speaking through Ezekiel about the people of Israel.

"They shall forget their shame and all the treachery they have practiced against me, when they dwell securely in their land with none to make them afraid, when I have brought them back from the peoples and gathered them from their enemies' lands, and through them have vindicated my holiness in the sight of many nations."

Ezekiel 39:26-27

Dear Lord, today I come to you in praise and thanksgiving. All of us have many past sins. You have been a loving God. You have forgiven us for our past bad behavior. When we now follow you, you keep us secure in our homes and in our land. Again Lord, I thank you for keeping us safe, and I praise you for the secure life you have provided. Keep us safe, Lord, as we worship you. Amen.

August 24

God is speaking to Daniel in a vision.

"Then he said to me, 'Fear not, Daniel, for from the first day that you set your heart to understand and humbled yourself before your God, your words have been heard, and I have come because of your words..."

Daniel 10:12

Dear Lord, I will always praise you. I try to remain humble before you and man. You have given me strength and courage. As I watch many people in this world turn away from you, I will walk towards you. Guide me please. I thank you for staying by my side. Amen.

August 25

A vision of God appearing as a man spoke to Daniel.

"Again one having the appearance of a man touched me and strengthened me. And he said, 'O man greatly loved, fear not, peace be with you; be strong and of good courage.' And as he spoke to me, I was strengthened and said, 'Let my lord speak, for you have strengthened me.'"

Daniel 10:18-19

Dear Lord, please bring me peace in this hectic world. I praise you and know that you are in control. I believe that those who follow you and live by your word will be blessed. I pray you count me among the blessed. I thank you for everything in my life. Amen.

August 26

God is speaking to Daniel.

"With a large army he will stir up his strength and courage against the king of the South. The king of the South will wage war with a large and very powerful army, but he will not be able to stand because of the plots devised against him ..."

Daniel 11:25

Dear Lord, even if the odds are against me, I can stand firm. Often situations seem impossible. But you can give me courage and strength. I can overcome any odds to be a winner. I have a very powerful team mate. I believe that I am oft times a winner just for showing up for the battle. Help me Lord to always be a good sport. I praise you and thank you Lord, for helping me to be strong even in my humility and submission. Amen.

August 27

God is speaking through his prophet Joel.

"Fear not, O land; be glad and rejoice, for the Lord has done great things!"

Joel 2:21

Dear Lord, I praise you always. When disasters occur, you are to be praised. When there is recovery from disaster, you deserve the praise. When I turn to you, you will always be there. I thank you Lord for the courage to go through whatever disaster or good time that comes my way. Amen.

August 28

God is speaking through his prophet Joel.

"Fear not, you beasts of the field, for the pastures of the wilderness are green; the tree bears its fruit; the fig tree and vine give their full yield."

Joel 2:22

Dear Lord, I thank you for all the abundance of food. I thank you for the green fields. I thank you for the safety of my animals. I praise you for the rain when it is needed. I praise you for your wondrous blessings. I know that you are the Lord. Please bless my family. Amen.

August 29

Jonah has been called to be a prophet, but Jonah is fleeing from the Lord.

"The sea was getting rougher and rougher. So they asked him, 'What should we do to make the sea calm down for us?' 'Pick me up and throw me into the sea,' he replied, 'and it will become calm. I know that it is my fault that this great storm has come upon you.'"

Jonah 1:11-12 NIV

Dear Lord, Jonah was running from you. You called him to serve and he turned his back on you. I know that I cannot run from you. My sins cannot escape you. When I sin, however small, I am running from you. If I feel fear or anxiety, the only thing that can calm me, is to turn away from any sin, ask forgiveness and come back to you. I thank you Lord, in advance for forgiveness. Amen.

August 30

God is speaking through Micah.

"He shall judge between many peoples, and shall decide disputes for strong nations far away; and they shall beat their swords into plowshares, and their spears into pruning hooks; nation shall not lift up sword against nation, neither shall they learn war anymore; but they shall sit every man under his vine and under his fig tree, and no one shall make them afraid, for the mouth of the Lord of hosts has spoken."

Micah 4:3-4

Dear Lord, as I try to walk in your path, may I find peace. I will not feel fear. May peace spread from under the vine, under the fig tree, on the farm, in the cities, then throughout the country and throughout the world. Even as wars may continue, may peace find your people. Amen.

August 31

Micah is speaking about messages from the Lord about a new ruler.

"And he shall stand and shepherd his flock in the strength of the Lord, in the majesty of the name of the Lord his God. And they shall dwell secure, for now he shall be great to the ends of the earth. And he shall be their peace."

Micah 5:4-5

Dear Lord, I praise you for the strength you have given me. I thank you for shepherding me when needed. I can count on you to lead me to a safe place if I wander out of your shelter. I always want to be near you Lord, but if I should be lost, even for a very short while, please find me and usher me back to your safety. I thank you for always staying close to me, even if I start to roam. I treasure your enduring love. Amen.

September 1

This is the prophet Habakkuk's prayer of praise.

"God, the Lord, is my strength; he makes my feet like the deer's; he makes me tread on my high places. To the choirmaster: with stringed instruments."

Habakkuk 3:19

Dear Lord, you are my strength. You are with me when I am athletic. You help me to run, move quickly, and sometimes even win various sporting games. I am a senior citizen and not a great athlete. When I play well, I rejoice. I love watching the professional athletes perform. They are often spectacular. I hope all the world's great, talented athletes always remember that their gifts come from you. Amen.

Fear Not

September 2

Zephaniah promises that God would bring his people home.

"... But I will leave in your midst a people humble and lowly. They shall seek refuge in the name of the Lord, those who are left in Israel; they shall do no injustice and speak no lies, nor shall there be found in their mouth a deceitful tongue. For they shall graze and lie down, and none shall make them afraid."

Zephaniah 3:12-13

Dear Lord, I praise your word which has shown me that when men turn away from you, trouble comes. But when men turn toward you, you give them comfort. Has our country turned away from you? If each of us would turn toward you, our country and the world might have less trouble. As for me, Lord, I will turn toward you. I look to you for comfort. None will make me afraid. I will try to share my attitude with others, so they too may lie down and be free from worries. I thank you, Lord, for your blessings. Amen

September 3

Zephaniah promises that God would bring his people home.

"The Lord has taken away the judgments against you; he has cleared away your enemies. The King of Israel, the Lord, is in your midst; you shall never again fear evil."

Zephaniah 3:15

Dear Lord, I praise you. I love you and thank you for all my blessings. You have taken my enemies far from me. You have given me a peaceful place to live. My life is peaceful. You are the reason. Stay with me Lord. Please let me walk beside you always. Amen.

September 4

Zephaniah promises that God would bring his people home.

"On that day it shall be said to Jerusalem: "Fear not, O Zion; let not your hands grow weak"

Zephaniah 3:16

Dear Lord, you are with me. I praise you. You make me happy. You fill me with quiet love. The world may be suffering, but I am singing a joyful song of praise. You alone can turn sadness into rejoicing. I thank you for that. I will try to always follow you Lord. Amen

September 5

God is speaking through Haggai about building a new house of worship.

"Yet now be strong, O Zerubbabel, declares the Lord. Be strong, O Joshua, son of Jehozadak, the high priest. Be strong, all you people of the land, declares the Lord. Work, for I am with you, declares the Lord of hosts, according to the covenant that I made with you when you came out of Egypt. My Spirit remains in your midst. Fear not."

Haggai 2:4-5

Dear Lord, I praise you. I thank you for reminding me to be brave and strong. You also reminded me in your word that everything on this earth is yours. The silver, gold, gems, oil, all valuable things are yours. All my possessions are yours. My children and my pets are yours. I am yours. I will honor you and worship you. You will stay by my side. This is a comforting relationship for me. Once again I thank you for my strength, bravery, comfort and peace. Amen.

September 6

God is speaking through the prophet Zechariah, telling the people of Jerusalem to obey him and receive his blessings as they rebuild the house of worship.

"... And as l you have been a byword of cursing among the nations, O house of Judah and house of Israel, so will I save you, and you shall be a blessing. Fear not, but let your hands be strong."

Zechariah 8:13

Dear Lord, in your words you have asked man to speak the truth and make peace. You ask for leaders of nations to come together and speak peace. May today's world leaders seek your advice and not be afraid. I praise you, Lord. As for me, I will try to always speak the truth and work for peace in my life. Help me to stay healthy and physically strong, so I may go on to do your work on earth. I thank you for my strong hands. Amen.

September 7

God is speaking through the prophet Zechariah, telling the people of Jerusalem to obey him and receive his blessings as they rebuild the house of worship.

"For thus says the Lord of hosts: 'As I purposed to bring disaster to you when your fathers provoked me to wrath, and I did not relent, says the Lord of hosts, so again have I purposed in these days to bring good to Jerusalem and to the house of Judah; fear not...'"

Zechariah 8:14-15

Dear Lord, I praise you. I am grateful that you can forgive sins of the past. You will bring good things to those who give up sinful ways and turn to you. I will try to follow your path and know that I will continue to receive your blessings. Then I can feel safe and secure. I will have nothing to fear. I thank you for being with me. Amen.

September 8

God is speaking through the prophet Zechariah saying he will care for Judah.

" '... I will make them strong in the Lord, and they shall walk in his name,' declares the Lord."

Zechariah 10:12

Dear Lord, walking in your name is a very important job. If I represent you on earth, I must hold myself to a very high standard. Of course, I can only be a mortal person, full of sin even as I try to live according to your word. But help me to remember that every small action in my daily life reflects you. You are there in all the small details of our lives. I will try to always walk in strength because I belong to you. I will think of you if insignificant things bother me. I will think of you as important events happen. You are involved in all things. I thank you for everything in my life. Amen.

September 9

This is the story of Joseph and Mary before the birth of Jesus when he considered that Mary was with child, and he had not been intimate with her. He had decided to quietly divorce her.

"But as he considered these things, behold, an angel of the Lord appeared to him in a dream, saying, 'Joseph, son of David, do not fear to take Mary as your wife, for that which is conceived in her is from the Holy Spirit...'"

Matthew 1:20

Dear Lord, I praise you. I thank you for my blessings. Because you are so great, I will not fear what people think. I will only concern myself with what you think. You may ask me to go against convention at times. I will be brave and follow you, Lord. I will try to pay attention to my dreams. I will listen quietly for your voice. I seek guidance from the Holy Spirit. Amen.

Fear Not

Jesus is speaking. This is a classic Bible chapter on anxiety and worry.

"Therefore I tell you, do not be anxious about your life, what you will eat or what you will drink, nor about your body, what you will put on. Is not life more than food, and the body more than clothing?"

Matthew 6:25

Dear Lord, I love you. I praise you and I know that you will care for me. I thank you for meeting my needs. You always do. Obviously my needs have been met because I am here today, alive and well. Remind me not to worry about money. Remind me not to be concerned about the national or world economy. Any money or possessions I have come from you. I will seek you, and I will have what I need. I will remember that you provide all I need, not all I want. You know what to provide for your children. As Jesus teaches, I will pray. Amen.

September 11

Jesus continues speaking.

"Look at the birds of the air: they neither sow nor reap nor gather into barns, and yet your heavenly Father feeds them. Are you not of more value than they? And which of you by being anxious can add a single hour to his span of life?"

Matthew 6:26-27

Dear heavenly Father, I am in awe of you. I know that only you know when any of us will be born or die. Only you know how many more days we have on earth. Only you can keep us safe. In today's world I need to rely on you. I will seek you and be secure as I walk with you. Today's world offers little else to rely on. Amen.

September 12

Jesus continues speaking.

"And why are you anxious about clothing?
Consider the lilies of the field, how they grow: they
neither toil nor spin, yet I tell you, even Solomon in
all his glory was not arrayed like one of these. But
if God so clothes the grass of the field, which today
is alive and tomorrow is thrown into the oven, will
he not much more clothe you, O you of little faith?"

Matthew 6:28-30

Dear Lord, I know you provide for me in time and
in abundance. You may not give me everything I
want, but you will give me what I need. I might not
have the most expensive designer clothes, but I will
have the clothes I need to be properly dressed. That
is why you are so great, Lord. It is wonderful to
know you will not leave me. All I have comes from
you. I love you, Lord Jesus. Amen.

Sept 13

Jesus continues speaking.

"Therefore do not be anxious, saying, 'What shall we eat?' or 'What shall we drink?' or 'What shall we wear?' For the Gentiles seek after all these things, and your heavenly Father knows that you need them all. But seek first the kingdom of God and his righteousness, and all these things will be added to you.''''"

Matthew 6:31-33

Dear Lord, you are awesome. I praise you for always providing us with food. Our country has an abundance of food. Too much food is probably more of a problem than not enough. Let me hear this message of Jesus and know that everything I have comes from you and you will continue to provide.. I thank you Lord, for always taking care of me. Amen.

September 14

Jesus continues speaking.

"Therefore do not be anxious about tomorrow, for tomorrow will be anxious for itself. Sufficient for the day is its own trouble."

Matthew 6:34

Dear Lord, I give you thanks and I give you praise for all things. I know all my blessings come from you. When I have concerns I will pray instead of worrying. Prayer is better. You are the greatest power. In you I put my trust. I will live today as it comes, enjoying today. Tomorrow will come tomorrow and then I will live it with your help. Amen.

September 15

Jesus is speaking to his apostles on a boat during a storm. They ask Jesus to save them.

"And he said to them, 'Why are you afraid, O you of little faith?' Then he rose and rebuked the winds and the sea, and l there was a great calm.'"

Matthew 8:26

Dear Lord, you are so wonderful. Help me to always have faith. Sometimes the influences of the world weigh me down and my faith wavers a little. Then I feel fear. Please help me not to be of little faith. Jesus, you can calm the seas. Surely you can bring a great calm over my mind when I forget my faith and feel anxiety. Please stay with me as I walk with you. You are an awesome force for peace. I thank you Lord. Amen.

September 16

Jesus speaks to a paralyzed man whom he is about to heal.

"Some people soon brought to him a crippled man lying on a mat. When Jesus saw how much faith they had, he said to the crippled man, 'My friend, don't worry! Your sins are forgiven.'"

Matthew 9:2 CEV

Dear Lord, I thank you for sacrificing your only son so our sins can be forgiven. We all sin. If I am human, I sin. But I can come to you with a faithful heart that asks for forgiveness, and my sins are wiped away. I have learned that some poor choices carry consequences, but you Lord, forgive me. I have faith that you love me enough to not expect me to be perfect as long as I am mortal. I will try to walk in your path and always ask for divine guidance. If I am stubborn, or lack faith, and do not listen to your word, help me to come to you with a sincere heart and ask you to forgive me my sins. In your name I ask for forgiveness. Amen.

Fear Not

September 17

Jesus is speaking to the woman with a bleeding problem who touches his garment and asks to be healed.

"Jesus turned. He saw the woman and said, 'Don't worry! You are now well because of your faith.' At that moment she was healed.'"

Matthew 9:22 CEV

Dear Lord, I thank you for your great power. I thank you Jesus for your wondrous healing. You are the Great Physician. You have healed me personally in times of illness. At other times, the doctors gave me medicines or performed surgery, but you were there with comfort. You eased the pain. You managed the fear. You worked through the hands of the medical professionals. Faith is in fact a great healer. I praise you Lord. I thank you for being with your children when they are healthy and when they are suffering with health concerns. No one can be truly healed without your help. Amen.

Fear Not

September 18

Jesus is speaking to his twelve disciples about persecution as he sends them out.

"Beware of men, for they will deliver you over to courts and flog you in their synagogues, and you will be dragged before governors and kings for my sake, to bear witness before them and the Gentiles. When they deliver you over, do not be anxious how you are to speak or what you are to say, for what you are to say will be given to you in that hour. For it is not you who speak, but the Spirit of your Father speaking through you."

Matthew 10:17-20

Dear Lord, in my daily life, I have many opportunities to offer words of faith to people I speak with. I do not share the gospel with those people as often as I could because of insecurity. I humbly ask you, Lord, to give me the words to be an effective ambassador of your word. Amen.

Fear Not

September 19

Jesus is speaking to his twelve disciples about persecution as he sends them out.

"So have no fear of them, for nothing is covered that will not be revealed, or hidden that will not be known."

Matthew 10:26

Dear Lord, you are so awesome. You know everything. You see everything. You show others what they need to see. You go with your followers. You are there in the darkness of the night. You protect them. I can hide nothing from you. Still, I feel safe with you by my side. Amen.

Fear Not

September 20

Jesus is speaking to his twelve disciples about persecution as he sends them out.

"And do not fear those who kill the body but cannot kill the soul. Rather fear him who can destroy both soul and body in hell."

Matthew 10:28

Dear Lord, I will always praise you and thank you for all my blessings. You have created everlasting life available to anyone who believes in you, your son, and asks. This is a very comforting gift. Help me to truly believe and truly know that whatever happens to me and my body on earth, my soul will live. This earth tempts us all away from our beliefs. There are a lot of evil forces coming against me and all of us. Please keep us safe, Lord. Hold me in your loving arms. Amen.

Fear Not

September 21

Jesus is speaking to his twelve disciples about persecution as he sends them out.

"Are not two sparrows sold for a penny? And not one of them will fall to the ground apart from your Father. But even the hairs of your head are all numbered. Fear not, therefore; you are of more value than many sparrows."

Matthew 10:29-31

Dear Lord, you are everything to me. Furthermore, I am important to you. Amazingly, you know the number of hairs on my head. You knew that before I was born. You will keep me in your care. Nothing will happen to me that you don't know about. You are my security. I will let you lead me. I will follow your path. I thank you, Lord, for offering me true comfort. I thank you for making me your child. Amen.

September 22

Jesus tells the parable of the sower who planted seeds among the thorns. The seeds grew but were choked out by the thorns.

"The seeds that fell among the thorn bushes are also people who hear the message. But they start worrying about the needs of this life and are fooled by the desire to get rich. So the message gets choked out, and they never produce anything."

Matthew 13:22 CEV

Dear Lord, you have asked me not to worry. You have especially asked me not to worry about money. Please give me the strength to obey your words. Please help me to be a productive citizen of your kingdom. Don't let worries about material things take my focus off of you, Lord. Please continue to bless me as I thank you for your words. I pray they fall on fertile ground. Amen.

September 23

Jesus is speaking to the disciples after he walked on water.

"But immediately Jesus spoke to them, saying, 'Take heart; it is I. Do not be afraid.'"

Matthew 14:27 ESV

Dear Lord, you can do amazing things. Your miracles are awesome. I thank you for these things. I will try to always have faith that even the supernatural is possible. You can do all things. I can do all things if you go with me. I thank you Lord. Peace in today's world seems impossible. Only with you can peace be accomplished. Amen.

Fear Not

Sept 24

Jesus is talking to Peter, James and John, his brother, after Jesus has been transfigured.

"But Jesus came and touched them, saying, 'Rise, and have no fear.'"

Matthew 17:7 ESV

Dear Lord, you alone give me strength and courage. With your help I can face all the difficult things in this world. I will be brave and strong. I praise you Lord, and thank you for the blessing of my courage. It came from you. Amen.

Fear Not

September 25

Jesus is speaking to the disciples.

"And you will hear of wars and rumors of wars. See that you are not alarmed, for this must take place, but the end is not yet."

Matthew 24:6 ESV

Dear Lord, your words mean a great deal to me. I want to praise you and thank you for being my strength. The news today can be disturbing. The media is out of control. Politicians and political candidates promise they can end violence and wars. We, on the other hand, might feel like the world as we know it is about to end. But your words, Jesus, remind me that only you are in control. I am comforted. I thank you again for being in my life and being in control. I will stay close and be still. Amen.

September 26

At the tomb of Jesus an angel speaks to Mary Magdalene, Mary mother of Jesus, and Joseph.

"But the angel said to the women, "Do not be afraid, for I know that you seek Jesus who was crucified..."

Matthew 28:5

Dear Lord, I praise you and thank you for sending your only son to earth for our salvation. I look to you, your son and the holy spirit, who are all one, for my comfort. Wild things happen on earth: hurricanes, floods, earthquakes. You have a beautiful plan that only you understand. But if I accept that only you are in control, then it is simple. I thank you so much for your scripture that says, "I am with you always, to the end of the age." Amen.

Matthew 28:20, ESV

Fear Not

September 27

Jesus is talking to the disciples after he has risen.

"Then Jesus said to them, 'Do not be afraid; go and tell my brothers to go to Galilee, and there they will see me.'"

Matthew 28:10

Dear Jesus, today I imagine meeting you along the road. You would accompany me on my journey. You would tell me, "Do not be afraid." I would listen to you and trust you. I will hear your voice as I walk through today's chaotic world. You will say, "Do not be afraid." I thank you, Lord, for those words. I praise you. Amen.

September 28

Jesus tells the parable of the seeds, planted among thorns, which grow and are then choked out by the fast growing thorns.

"The seeds that fell among the thorn bushes are also people who hear the message. But they start worrying about the needs of this life. They are fooled by the desire to get rich and to have all kinds of other things. So the message gets choked out, and they never produce anything."

Mark 4:18-19 CEV

Dear Lord, please do not let the worries of this world keep me from focusing on a God centered life. I want to spend my emotional energy seeking you. I want to pay attention only to what is good, pure, lovely and holy. Please help me to do this. I am human, and my brain likes to wander and sometimes get filled with thoughts that are not productive. I want to work for you, serve your kingdom and be a light to the people I come in daily contact with. If I focus on this I know all my needs will be met. I need you there helping me. Amen

September 29

Jesus is out to sea with the disciples and he calms the storm.

"And he awoke and rebuked the wind and said to the sea, 'Peace! Be still!' And the wind ceased, and there was a great calm. He said to them, 'Why are you so afraid? Have you still no faith?'"

Mark 4:39-40

Dear Lord, I thank you for your words of comfort. Your words, "Peace! Be Still!" have helped me through great personal heartbreak. My stomach was churning like the ocean. Those three words calmed me. When I feel afraid, I might forget my faith. Lord, please increase my faith as I turn to you daily with praise and thanks in my heart. Amen.

September 30

Jesus is speaking to Jairus, a ruler, who is being told that his daughter is dead.

"But overhearing what they said, Jesus said to the ruler of the synagogue, "Do not fear, only believe."

Mark 5:36

Dear Lord, in your holy words you commanded, "Do not fear, only believe." Oh, if it were only that easy! My faith is always being tested. I live in a scary world. Please help me, Lord, to have a believer's heart and a lion's spirit. I praise you for the world you created. Even though there is much violence around me, I know this is your world. You are in control. You can help me have both faith and courage because as your servant I ask this of you. I thank you for being in charge. I thank you for managing my life and helping me to believe. Amen.

October 1

Jesus talks to the disciples as they watch him walk on water.

"And he saw they were making headway painfully for the wind was against them. And about the fourth watch of the night he came to them, walking on the sea. He meant to pass by them, but when they saw him walking on the sea they thought it was a ghost, and cried out, for they all saw him and were terrified. But immediately he spoke to them and said, "Take heart; it is I. Do not be afraid."

Mark 6:48-50

Dear Lord, you are so great. I praise you for your continual love. When I see signs of your power and greatness, I will not be afraid. I will love you rather than fear you, but I know I must follow your ways and do my best to obey you. I want to please you. I thank you for being there for me and comforting me when things of the world feel overwhelming. Amen.

October 2

Jesus is speaking.

"Many will come in my name, saying, 'I am he!' and they will lead many astray. And when you hear of wars and rumors of wars, do not be alarmed. This must take place, but the end is not yet".

Mark 13:6-7

Dear Lord, I praise you and know that you are in control. I am thankful for that. Mortals cannot control all the strife in the world. Even those in the military can try only to control their small space. You know when wars will start, when they will end, and who will be the victor. Politicians and the media use talk of wars to their advantage. I will not be alarmed. I will pray to you. I will go out into the world today and try to be an example of optimism You have given me a spirit of courage. I will relax and be happy. I thank you, Lord, for the peace. Amen.

Fear Not

October 3

Jesus is speaking to Peter, James, John and Andrew on the Mount of Olives.

"And when they bring you to trial and deliver you over, do not be anxious beforehand what you are to say, but say whatever is given you in that hour, for it is not you who speak, but the Holy Spirit."

Mark 13:11

Dear Lord, I will praise you continually. I thank you for all my blessings. As I try to share my love of you, I will not be worried about what others think about my love of the Lord. I will be enthusiastic about you, God. I will try to be joyous and let your light shine through me. My words will not be my own. They will be supplied by the Holy Spirit. If they are to be welcomed by others, that will come from you. My courage to speak will be supplied by you. Amen.

October 4

Mark tells of events following the death of Jesus.

"And when evening had come, since it was the day of Preparation, that is, the day before the Sabbath, Joseph of Arimathea, a respected member of the council, who was also himself looking for the kingdom of God, took courage and went to Pilate and asked for the body of Jesus."

Mark 15:42-43

Dear Lord, I praise you and thank you for the gospels. In this scripture, Joseph had to do something difficult and possibly dangerous. He could face dire consequences, but he went bravely to the authorities and asked for what he wanted. I will always submit to you, Lord, but there are times in the world where I need to be assertive. If it is necessary, I pray you will give me the strength and courage to do what I must. I know you will be with me. Amen.

October 5

An angel at Jesus' tomb speaks to Mary Magdalene, Mary, mother of James, and Salome.

"And he said to them, 'Do not be alarmed. You seek Jesus of Nazareth, who was crucified. He has risen; he is not here. See the place where they laid him...'"

Mark 16:6

Dear heavenly father, some days it feels like you and your son are not here. There are so many shootings and riots in our country. There is so much hatred, bigotry, injustice. But I know that you are here on earth and in your heavenly throne. So I remember to praise you. Your word says, "In everything give thanks." (Thessalonians 5:18) You are in control. That is my comfort. Please help me to always feel your presence. Please keep me safe in your world. Amen.

October 6

An angel is speaking to Zechariah about the pregnancy of his wife, Elizabeth, with the baby who is to become John the Baptist.

"But the angel said to him, "Do not be afraid, Zechariah, for your prayer has been heard, and your wife Elizabeth will bear you a son, and you shall call his name John..."

Luke 1:13

Dear Lord, let me not be afraid in your presence. You are great and all powerful. Sometimes the way you work in this world can seem overwhelming. Please help me to follow you. Let me simply love you, praise you, thank you and believe you are in control. If I hear your voice, let me listen. Let me be courageous in sharing your word. When I need encouragement, please send your angels to surround me with your peace. Amen.

Fear Not

October 7

An angel announces to Mary the conception of Jesus from the Lord.

"And the angel said to her, 'Do not be afraid, Mary, for you have found favor with God ...'"

Luke 1:30

Dear Lord, your miracles are many. Often it is hard for me to find miracles like the ones in the Bible. If today an angel came to speak to me, I might not recognize him. Please help me to open my eyes and my mind to your great miracles. All around me in nature I see your miracles. In birth of babies, I see your miracles. My very life is a miracle. Thank you for giving me life, and always being in it. Amen.

October 8

Zechariah speaks upon the birth of his son, John the Baptist.

"Blessed be the Lord God of Israel, for he has visited and redeemed his people and has raised up a horn of salvation for us in the house of his servant David, as he spoke by the mouth of his holy prophets from of old, that we should be saved from our enemies and from the hand of all who hate us; to show the mercy promised to our fathers and to remember his holy covenant, the oath that he swore to our father Abraham, to grant us that we, being delivered from the hand of our enemies, might serve him without fear, in holiness and righteousness before him all our days... '"

Luke 1:68-75

Dear Lord, I repeat the prayer of Zechariah. Please be with our nation in times of peace and in times of turmoil. Only you can grant us salvation. Amen.

October 9

An angel announces the birth of Jesus to the shepherds.

"And the angel said to them, 'Fear not, for behold, I bring you good news of great joy that will be for all the people ...'"

Luke 2:10

Dear Lord, I praise you for giving us your son. I thank you for the peace you place in our hearts. Lots of angels surround the people involved in the story of the coming of Jesus. It is reported that the people always feel fear when the angels speak to them. Then the angels say, "Fear not." Please send some of those angels to earth today to calm the planet. I pray for more peace on our planet if it is your will. Please help me to place any worry or burden on Jesus' shoulders. Today we need peace on earth and in our country. Amen.

Fear Not

October 10

Jesus' parents find him teaching in the temple.

"When his parents found him, they were amazed. His mother said, 'Son, why have you done this to us? Your father and I have been very worried, and we have been searching for you!' Jesus answered, 'Why did you have to look for me? Didn't you know that I would be in my Father's house?'"

Luke 2:48-49 CEV

Dear Lord, I can only begin to imagine the fear Mary and Joseph felt when they thought they lost their son. Some things are so horrible that anyone would be full of fear. But Jesus was in his father's house. If the worst, most unthinkable things were to happen to our loved ones, we could eventually rest assured that they are in their father's house. That wouldn't be much help at the time, but it is true. Please comfort all those that lose loved ones. Keep their faith strong. Amen.

October 11

Jesus is teaching the people from a boat.

"For he and all who were with him were astonished at the catch of fish that they had taken, and so also were James and John, sons of Zebedee, who were partners with Simon. And Jesus said to Simon, "Do not be afraid; from now on you will be catching men."

Luke 5:9-10

Dear Lord, I praise you. I thank you for my life. I am thankful for the lakes and oceans you created, and the opportunity to relax and go fishing. Lord, please help me also to be a fisher of men. Your seas are mighty. I am small. Please keep me safe in your waters. Keep me safe in this perilous world, as I go out and try to do your will in this crazy place. Amen.

October 12

Jesus explains the parable of the sower. The seeds planted among the thorns sprout the but the fast growing thorns choke them out.

"The seeds that fell among thorn bushes stand for those who hear; but the worries and riches and pleasures of this life crowd in and choke them, and their fruit never ripens."

Luke 8:14 GNT

Dear Lord, please help me to grow in faith and devotion. Do not let worries about money and good times take my attention away from worshiping you. Let the joys of the kingdom be greater than pleasures on earth. As I go about living a life for you, I know I am filled with continual joy. Faith and hope can make a person feel very happy. Cares about the world cannot bring joy and happiness. Lead me in your bright path while I enjoy my life you gave to me, Lord. Amen.

October 13

Jesus calms the storm.

"And they went and woke him, saying, 'Master, Master, we are perishing!' And he awoke and rebuked the wind and the raging waves, and they ceased, and there was a calm."

Luke 8:24

Dear Lord, if you can calm the seas, the skies, the storms, surely you can calm my heart. Please remove worry and strife from my thoughts. Take the drama out of my life. As life's storms occur, let me handle them calmly, knowing that you are in control. I know that life's crisis do not last forever. I can wait patiently and know that you are the Lord. Calm will be restored. I praise you and thank you for your power. Amen.

October 14

Jesus speaks after he calms the storm.

"He said to them, 'Where is your faith?' And they were afraid, and they marveled, saying to one another, 'Who then is this, that he commands even winds and water, and they obey him?'"

Luke 8:25

Dear Lord, I want to increase my faith. As I strive to live a life free from fear and worry, I have learned that it is impossible without faith. I have learned this by studying the words of God, the father, and the words of Jesus as written in the Bible. I need your help, Lord, on this journey towards courage and absolute faith. I know you are there hearing my prayers. I praise you and thank you for everything. Amen.

October 15

Jesus is speaking to the ruler, Jairus, about his daughter who is reported to be dead.

"But Jesus on hearing this answered him, 'Do not fear; only believe, and she will be well.'"

Luke 8:50

Dear Lord, your power is so great that even death cannot defy you. You are in control. I praise you. I thank you for my life and my belief. It is so simple. "Do not fear, only believe." You have said that before. It can change lives. Keep me close Lord and nourish my belief. I pray in your son's name. Amen.

October 16

Luke tells the story of Mary and Martha.

"The Lord and his disciples were traveling along and came to a village. When they got there, a woman named Martha welcomed him into her home. She had a sister named Mary, who sat down in front of the Lord and was listening to what he said. Martha was worried about all that had to be done. Finally, she went to Jesus and said, 'Lord, doesn't it bother you that my sister has left me to do all the work by myself? Tell her to come and help me!'"

The Lord answered, "Martha, Martha! You are worried and upset about so many things, but only one thing is necessary. Mary has chosen what is best, and it will not be taken away from her."

Luke 10:38-42 CEV

Dear Lord, at times I need to rest and hear your voice. Amen.

Fear Not

October 17

Jesus speaks to his disciples as a large crowd gathers.

"I tell you, my friends, do not fear those who kill the body, and after that have nothing more that they can do."

Luke 12:4

Dear Lord, I praise you. I thank you for all the long days you have allowed my body to remain here on earth. You have watched me sin, and then showed me your forgiveness. My body will not always be here on earth. But that is not something to ever be fearful about. Please, Lord, help me to truly understand that. Help me to know these things in my heart and just believe. Then as I grow older, as remaining days grow shorter, and as the world grows more dangerous, I will not fear. Lord, protect my soul. Let the Holy Spirit live and shine in me. Amen.

Fear Not

October 18

Jesus speaks to his disciples about how much God values each of us.

"Are not five sparrows sold for two pennies? And not one of them is forgotten before God. Why, even the hairs of your head are all numbered. Fear not; you are of more value than many sparrows."

Luke 12:6-7

Dear Lord, I praise you for all your creation. You made everything. You are in charge of it all. I thank you for my life. I belong to you. You know all about me. You were there when I was born. You know how many days I have on earth. You provide for all creatures here on earth. Surely you will provide for me. I have nothing to fear because you love me and you want to take care of me. You alone are most capable. Again I thank you, Lord. Amen.

October 19

Jesus is speaking about acknowledging him.

"... And when they bring you before the synagogues and the rulers and the authorities, do not be anxious about how you should defend yourself or what you should say, for the Holy Spirit will teach you in that very hour what you ought to say."

Luke 12:11-12

Dear Lord, today I am thinking about anxiety. You are the only real cure for that. Many are terribly afraid of speaking in public. Many are anxious about speaking to the police, school officials or church officials. I ask you to let the Holy Spirit lead me. I praise the Holy Spirit in advance for bringing the correct words into my mouth, for giving me the courage to speak and act on God's behalf. I thank you and praise you, Lord. Amen.

Fear Not

October 20

Jesus speaks to the disciples about not worrying.

"And he said to his disciples, 'Therefore I tell you, do not be anxious about your life, what you will eat, nor about your body, what you will put on ...'"

Luke 12:22

Dear Lord, I praise you today. I praise your holy word that is so full of inspiration on knowing that you will supply our needs. In these uncertain political times, the country feels unstable. The violence of today makes the future seem unclear. But you feed the birds and clothe the flowers. Surely you will always care for me. Thank you for everything in my life. Amen.

October 21

Jesus is speaking to the disciples about how useless it is to worry.

"Who of you by worrying can add a single hour to his life?"

Luke 12:25 NIV

Dear Lord, I thank you for the wisdom of your words. I thank you for the many days of life you have given me. I thank you for leading me to read the Bible and study your words of wisdom. Whenever I start feeling anxious about my age or how much longer I might live, I will praise you instead of worrying. I will praise you whenever I think about you. I will try to always keep you on my mind. You are my first love. Amen.

Fear Not

October 22

Jesus continues speaking to the disciples about the how useless it is to worry.

"Since you cannot do this very little thing, why do you worry about the rest?"

Luke 12:26 NIV

Dear Lord, I often think about the advice of a Christian friend. "If you are going to pray, don't worry. If you are going to worry, there is no need to pray. So you might as well pray." I think that is good advice that I try to follow. Please keep guiding me to turn towards you in praise and thanksgiving, instead of turning to myself with anxiety. Help me be strong. I am grateful for your help with this. I praise your steady love. Amen

October 23

Jesus continues speaking to the disciples about the how useless it is to worry.

"And do not seek what you are to eat and what you are to drink, nor be worried. For all the nations of the world seek after these things, and your Father knows that you need them. Instead, seek his kingdom, and these things will be added to you."

Luke 12:29-31

Dear Lord, your son's words say what I want to always remember. I thank you for sending him to comfort us. I know you will provide, so worrying shows that I'm not trusting you. Let me keep these verses in my heart as I worship you. Let me love you with all my mind, heart and soul. Please help me keep my focus on you. I know you provide what I need. I know that it's not always what I want. So I will trust you as my perfect heavenly father to know and do what is best. Amen.

October 24

Jesus continues speaking to the disciples about the how useless it is to worry.

"Fear not, little flock, for it is your Father's good pleasure to give you the kingdom."

Luke 12:32

Oh Lord, you are so wonderful. You are so generous. You have already given me so much. How could I ever doubt you will give me what I need in the future? It is you in my life that I truly need. When you are with me, I am safe. I am satisfied. I need for nothing. You are everything to me. I could walk away from everything else in my world, if I have you. Please give me the wisdom to stay in your graces, because I know you will always stay with me. Amen.

October 25

Jesus tells the parable of the persistent widow who benefitted by her persistence.

"And he spake a parable unto them to this end, that men ought always to pray, and not to faint;"

Luke 18:1 KJV

Dear Lord, I will try to be more faithful in praying continuously for your kingdom here on earth. I will try to spend more time in prayer. If I feel there is a legitimate need, I will bring it to you and pray continually. I will pray, not worry. I know your will be done. I will not lose heart of feel faint when terrible things happen. I will keep my faith and pray, pray, pray. I know you will answer in your own time and in your own way. I thank you and praise you. Amen.

Fear Not

October 26

Jesus answers the disciples questions about the coming end of time.

"And he said, 'See that you are not led astray. For many will come in my name, saying, 'I am he!' and, 'The time is at hand!' Do not go after them. And when you hear of wars and tumults, do not be terrified, for these things must first take place, but the end will not be at once.'"

Luke 21:8-9

Dear Lord, again your words provide comfort. This world, our country, and even our peaceful rural communities are seeing terrible violent acts occurring. Earthquakes, tornadoes and floods are constant threats. At times it is hard not to pay attention to the media. I have even heard religious leaders deliver terrible messages of doom. Help me remember only you are in control. Only you know the reason for what is happening. But I trust you. You give me strength. I offer prayers of peace to you. Amen.

October 27

Jesus speaks to the disciples questions about being persecuted by enemies.

"Don't worry about what you will say to defend yourselves. I will give you the wisdom to know what to say. None of your enemies will be able to oppose you or to say that you are wrong."

Luke 21:14-15 CEV

Dear Lord, I praise you for your justice. I thank you for the peace you offer me. Please continue to allow me to live a peaceful life. I pray that if I have any enemies you will turn them away from me. If I have every day, petty disagreements with people, please give me the words to act as your representative and never act in an unchristian way. Give me only words of peace, love and encouragement. I do not need to defend myself. You will defend me. Amen.

Fear Not

October 28

Jesus talks to the disciples questions about being persecuted due to their faith.

"But don't worry! You will be saved by being faithful to me."

Luke 21:18-19 CEV

Dear Lord, as I become a more loyal member of your kingdom, I will become more faithful to you. I will be strengthened. I will no longer trust in myself, but trust totally in you. Please give me the courage to always do your will. I can do anything when I have put my trust in Jesus to strengthen me. I praise and trust you, Lord. Amen.

October 29

Jesus speaks to the disciples about the returning of the Son of Man.

"And there will be signs in sun and moon and stars, and on the earth distress of nations in perplexity because of the roaring of the sea and the waves, people fainting with fear and with foreboding of what is coming on the world. For the powers of the heavens will be shaken. And then they will see the Son of Man coming in a cloud with power and great glory. Now when these things begin to take place, straighten up and raise your heads, because your redemption is drawing near."

Luke 21:25-28

Dear Lord, only you know the complete plan for man's salvation. We can only see things in finite terms. Stay with me until the end. I praise you, Lord. Amen.

October 30

Jesus continues telling the disciples about the coming end of times.

"Take care that your hearts aren't dulled by drinking parties, drunkenness, and the anxieties of day-to-day life. Don't let that day fall upon you unexpectedly, like a trap. It will come upon everyone who lives on the face of the whole earth. Stay alert at all times, praying that you are strong enough to escape everything that is about to happen and to stand before the Human One."

Luke 21:34-36 CEB

Dear Lord, I praise you and thank you for leading me on a more wholesome path today. Please don't allow me to slide back into behaviors that do not honor you. I will be strong with your help, and ready to face whatever comes my way. Amen.

October 31

Jesus prays on the Mount of Olives. He knows he is about to be imprisoned and crucified.

"And there appeared to him an angel from heaven, strengthening him."

Luke 22:43

Dear Lord, I pray that in times of crisis you will send an angel from heaven to strengthen me. I thank you in advance. I know you will care for me in any situation. Jesus turned to you as he fought his ultimate battle. His disciples were weary from grieving. But you stayed near and gave them courage. Because of you, Jesus, we are forgiven our sins and washed clean. I praise my Lord and Savior. Amen.

Fear Not

November 1

Jesus appears to the disciples after his crucifixion, death and resurrection.

"As they were talking about these things, Jesus himself stood among them, and said to them, 'Peace to you!' But they were startled and frightened and thought they saw a spirit. And he said to them, 'Why are you troubled, and why do doubts arise in your hearts?'"

Luke 24:36-38

Dear Lord, again you have asked that we not be troubled or afraid. I come to you as a child before my parents. If I have been disobedient, then I should be concerned. But if I have been obedient, then I must never be afraid. You are a loving Father. Jesus is a loving God. I am surrounded by love and protection. In this world I need that. I am grateful and I offer praise. Amen.

Fear Not

November 2

Jesus speaks to the disciples after they watch him walk on water.

"But he said to them, "It is I; do not be afraid."

John 6:20

Dear Lord, your powers are amazing. Jesus, you can walk on water! You, Lord, are the only force that needs to be feared, and that is only if I rise up against you, instead of choosing to walk beside you. I know I must believe in you, love you, and trust you. I must know your word and follow your simple commands. I must love my neighbor as myself. When I see your mighty presence, I will not be afraid. I will know that you are on my side. I thank you for that. I praise your name. Amen.

Fear Not

November 3

Jesus is riding a young donkey. He speaks to the disciples and a large crowd.

"Fear not, daughter of Zion; behold, your king is coming, sitting on a donkey's colt!"

John 12:15

Oh Dear Lord, today the world needs your message. Many walk in darkness. Jesus is the light. He has come. He is with us. There will always be darkness in the world. Let me walk in the light. With Jesus in my life, there is no fear. There is love. Hatred is darkness. Prejudice is darkness. Sin is darkness. Through thousands of years this doesn't change. Wars, prejudice, sin and hatred abound. But I choose the light. I will stay out of the darkness where trouble looms. I trust the Lord. I am thankful for the light. Amen.

November 4

Jesus is speaking to his disciples.

"Jesus said to his disciples, 'Don't be worried! Have faith in God and have faith in me. There are many rooms in my Father's house. I wouldn't tell you this, unless it was true. I am going there to prepare a place for each of you...'"

John 14:1-2 CEV

Dear Lord, I praise you and thank you for sending your only son to comfort us and show us the way. In Jesus' name I pray that one day I will see your face. It is simple, but not that simple. I must have faith. That is not always easy. I must know you. Jesus, I must know you. I must understand that you, the father, are the same as you, Jesus, the son, and that the Holy Spirit is one with you and lives in me. This is not so simple, but I will believe it as a child. I will come to the father through the son. That is the way. I must come with love, joy, hope and faith. Then I will have no fear or worry. Amen.

Fear Not

November 5

Jesus is speaking to the disciples.

"Peace I leave with you; my peace I give to you. Not as the world gives do I give to you. Let not your hearts be troubled, neither let them be afraid."

John 14:27

Dear Lord, I thank you for sending your son. I thank you for the peace your son offers us. I thank you for the peace that is greater than any peace found here on earth. I thank you for bringing peace to me. I praise you as I find my peace even when the whole world around me seems troubled. The Holy Spirit calms my heart as I hear about political struggles in my country. I am saddened but unafraid when I hear about mass shootings. I rest in the peace of Jesus when I know that wars are going on around me. I will remember Jesus' words, "Peace! be still!" Amen.

November 6

The Sanhedrin have been questioning Peter and John.

"Now when they saw the boldness of Peter and John, and perceived that they were uneducated, common men, they were astonished. And they recognized that they had been with Jesus."

Acts 4:13

Dear Lord, today I praise you for all the courage you are able to give to ordinary people. I personally tend to be timid and easy to frighten. But you, Jesus, have given me great strength and power over my fears. When I forget to trust in you and start to feel anxious, I remember how many times you tell your prophets and disciples not to be afraid. You are talking to me. I have been with you, therefore I am bold. Amen.

November 7

After Peter and John were released from prison, they went to their people and told what the Sanhedrin Chief Priests and elders said. The people prayed.

"And now, Lord, look upon their threats and grant to your servants to continue to speak your word with all boldness, while you stretch out your hand to heal, and signs and wonders are performed through the name of your holy servant Jesus."

Acts 4:29-30

Dear Lord, I praise you and thank you for letting me be one of your children. I need to ask that you please grant me the ability to speak your word with more boldness. I ask this because there are so many people in my circle of friends and family that so desperately need to hear it. Let the Holy Spirit give me the words, and open the hearts of all those to whom I speak. Amen.

November 8

The people prayed after Peter and John returned from prison. They were told what the Sanhedrin said.

"And when they had prayed, the place in which they were gathered together was shaken, and they were all filled with the Holy Spirit and continued to speak the word of God with boldness."

Acts 4:31

Dear Lord, I praise you and thank you for your presence in my life. Sometimes when I worship, I feel your closeness very strongly. I feel like I am filled with the Holy Spirit. Other times I just know you are there, being still. Let me be bold whether you are shouting with me, or speaking in a still small voice. Amen.

November 9

Saul becomes a disciple.

"But Barnabas took him and brought him to the apostles and declared to them how on the road he had seen the Lord, who spoke to him, and how at Damascus he had preached boldly in the name of Jesus."

Acts 9:27

Dear Lord, you performed bold miracles to Saul. Then Saul gained greater courage and wisdom in preaching the good news about Jesus. Please help give me that kind of courage. I do not need spectacular miracles to believe in you. I see the miracle of life and creation all around me. Help me to be a stronger disciple for you. Amen.

November 10

Saul becomes a disciple.

"So he went in and out among them at Jerusalem, preaching boldly in the name of the Lord."

Acts 9:28

Dear Lord, I praise you and I thank you for your word. I would love to go around preaching boldly for the Lord. But before I can do that, I need to have plenty of faith. I need to follow the correct path. Most importantly, I need a large dose of divine guidance. I need to spend more time studying your words. Then I need to listen to see what exactly you would like me to do in your kingdom. Sometimes it takes courage to just wait on you. Amen.

Fear Not

November 11

Three men sent by Cornelius are looking for Simon, called Peter. Peter has a vision. Then he is told that the men have come for him.

"While Peter was still thinking about the vision, the Holy Spirit said to him, "Three men are here looking for you. Hurry down and go with them. Don't worry, I sent them."

Acts 10:19-20 CEV

Dear Lord, I praise you. I thank you for sending the Holy Spirit as a guide. If I pay attention, and ask for divine guidance, I will not have to worry about what I should do. If I trust in you, and not my own understanding, I will make good decisions. You will take care of me. You will provide. I just need to listen. It is not always easy, so I must pray often and sincerely, with belief and thanksgiving. Then I turn it over to you and know that you are my guide. Amen.

November 12

Peter explains his actions.

"Just then three men who had been sent from Caesarea arrived at the house where we were staying. The Holy Spirit told me to go with them and not to worry that they were Gentiles. These six brothers here accompanied me, and we soon entered the home of the man who had sent for us. He told us how an angel had appeared to him in his home and had told him, 'Send messengers to Joppa, and summon a man named Simon Peter. He will tell you how you and everyone in your household can be saved!'"

Acts 11:11-14 NLT

Dear Lord, please give me the courage to follow the voice of the Holy Spirit. Allow me to trust you as my faith grows stronger. Please stay close to me. Amen.

November 13

Paul and Barnabas speak to Jews and Gentiles in Iconium on Paul's first missionary trip.

"So they remained for a long time, speaking boldly for the Lord, who bore witness to the word of his grace, granting signs and wonders to be done by their hands."

Acts 14:3

Dear Lord, I praise you and thank you for the grace you have shown me. Paul suffered greatly in order to preach his faith. I have never had to endure that kind of suffering. Maybe that is why I take my faith for granted sometimes. Lord, I ask you please to help me to grow closer to you, let my faith be stronger, and give me the words to speak courageously about the wonders of being a believer. Amen.

Fear Not

November 14

God is speaking to Paul in Corinth.

*"And the Lord said to Paul one night in m a vision,
'Do not be afraid, but go on speaking and do not be
silent, for I am with you, and no one will attack you
to harm you, for I have many in this city who are my
people.'"*

Acts 18:9-10

Dear Lord, I thank you for always being with me. I
thank you for your words of comfort. I thank you
for keeping me safe. You alone are my courage.
Please help me to always remember to praise you.
You are wondrous. Your word is amazing. Please
stay with me always, Lord. Amen.

November 15

Apollos, a Jewish man well versed in scripture, speaks boldly in the synagogue in Ephesus.

"He began to speak boldly in the synagogue, but when Priscilla and Aquila heard him, they took him aside and explained to him the way of God more accurately."

Acts 18:26

Dear Lord, I praise you. I thank you for everything I have. I thank you for everything I have learned. Help me to be humble and realize that I know very little about your ways. I am not smarter than anyone else. I do not know more than anyone else. All wisdom comes from you. All knowledge comes from you. If I speak boldly, please let me take care that my words come from you and that I am being led by the Holy Spirit. I can do nothing on my own. Amen.

November 16

Paul spent three months in Ephesus preaching the gospel of Jesus.

"And he entered the synagogue and for three months spoke boldly, reasoning and persuading them about the kingdom of God."

Acts 19:8

Dear Lord, you have given Paul great courage. He was tireless in spreading the good news of Jesus to his world. He travelled great distances. He suffered many hardships in order to keep on preaching the gospel. He was persistent. He never gave up. He never ran from a disagreement. He stood up for the truth even though many tried to quiet him. I ask you Lord, to let me learn from his wonderful example. Please keep giving me the strength I need to do your work. Amen.

November 17

Paul is speaking about a young man named Eutychus who fell into a deep sleep and fell out a window. He seemed to be dead.

"But Paul went down and bent over him, and taking him in his arms, said, 'Do not be alarmed, for his life is in him.'"

Acts 20:10

Dear Lord, I thank you for great miracles and everyday small miracles. You keep us healthy. You give our bodies healing power. You save some from death. It is all your will. No one stays on this earth forever, but all your children are continually wrapped in your comfort. I praise you. Amen.

Fear Not

November 18

Paul is on a ship sailing through a storm. The ship is heading toward Italy. Paul is speaking to the men on board.

"But now I urge you to keep up your courage, because not one of you will be lost; only the ship will be destroyed."

Acts 27:22 NIV

Dear Lord, today I drove through a hail storm. I worried that my truck would get dented. I have been in tornados and hurricanes. I have been through storms on boats. A few times I feared for my life. Most times I worried about my property. All our possessions are meaningless. They all come from you. Even if we worked hard to obtain them, our jobs came from you. Let me not be concerned for material things. Please give me the faith to know that with you I can weather any storm. Amen.

November 19

Paul is on the ship going towards Italy. There is a storm. An angel speaks to Paul. Paul is reporting this to the men on board.

"For this very night there stood before me an angel of the God to whom I belong and whom I worship, and he said, 'Do not be afraid, Paul; you must stand before Caesar. And behold, God has granted you all those who sail with you.' So take heart, men, for I have faith in God that it will be exactly as I have been told.'"

Acts 27:23-25

Dear Lord, I trust you. Help me always have faith and trust in you for the safety of me and those travelling with me. Protect those around me. I am always grateful for your love and protection you have given me all my life. I will stay with you forever. I thank you for being my strength and courage. Amen.

Fear Not

November 20

Paul arrives by ship in Rome to preach.

"And the brothers there, when they heard about us, came as far as the Forum of Appius and Three Taverns to meet us. On seeing them Paul thanked God and took courage."

Acts 28:15

Dear Lord, when Paul sees that he has survived prison and perilous sea journeys, he takes time to thank God. His faith in God has given him courage. He is now allowed to preach, but he is under guard. He doesn't complain about his situation. He gives thanks. Lord, help me to always see the positive side of life. Let me appreciate whatever circumstances I find myself in. It is always your will. I praise you and thank you for all you do in my life. Amen.

Fear Not

This is from the letters Paul wrote to the church in Rome.

"For all who are led by the Spirit of God are sons of God. For you did not receive the spirit of slavery to fall back into fear, but you have received the Spirit of adoption as sons, by whom we cry, 'Abba! Father!'"

Romans 8:14-15

Dear Lord, I am so grateful to have such a wondrous, loving father. You are always with me. You will always protect me. You will always provide. When the world around me gets crazy and I become concerned for my very survival, about my comfort, about my possessions, I stop and remember that you are my father. You are the most powerful. I love you. I thank you for having cared for me in the past. I thank you for caring for me in the future. In your son's name. Jesus, I pray. Amen.

Fear Not

November 22

Paul continues the letter written to the church in Rome.

"For rulers are not a terror to good conduct, but to bad. Would you have no fear of the one who is in authority? Then do what is good, and you will receive his approval, for he is God's servant for your good. But if you do wrong, be afraid, for he does not bear the sword in vain. For he is the servant of God, an avenger who carries out God's wrath on the wrongdoer."

Romans 13:3-4

Dear Lord, I only have the understanding of man, and you are God. Today, as in Paul's time, not all rulers or leaders are good. Some either have evil intentions, or make mistakes. But this word from Paul still makes sense. I will try to do what is right by God, and try to follow the laws of the land. If there is conflict, I will pray about it with a pure heart. Then I need not fear. I pray for wise and loving leaders. I know you are in total control. That gives me great peace. Amen.

November 23

Paul ministers to the Gentiles.

"But on some points I have written to you very boldly by way of reminder, because of the grace given me by God to be a minister of Christ Jesus to the Gentiles in the priestly service of the gospel of God, so that the offering of the Gentiles may be acceptable, sanctified by the Holy Spirit."

Romans 15:15-16

Dear Lord, Paul calls you the God of hope. Please God, fill me with joy and peace as I trust in you. Let me overflow with hope given to me by the power of the Holy Spirit. That is what Paul prayed for the Gentiles. Let that prayer apply to me today. As my hope is strong today, help me to build up those who may be weak. I praise you and thank you, Lord. Amen.

November 24

Paul writes about marriage in a letter to the church in Corinth.

"I want all of you to be free from worry. An unmarried man worries about how to please the Lord."

1 Corinthians 7:32 CEV

Dear Lord, I praise you. I thank you for the good relationships in my life. People spend a lot of energy on human relationships. I can become stressed with the people in my life when they do not act the way I want them to. It is not my job to control anyone's life, not even my own. That is your job, God. I will try to leave that job in your capable hands. I will not worry about other people. If I have concerns, I will pray, and give all problems to you. That will give me peace. I have you to thank for that peace. You must come first in all relationships. Help me to remember that always and keep my focus on you. Amen.

November 25

Paul writes a letter to the church in Corinth after his visit there.

"Therefore seeing we have this ministry, as we have received mercy, we faint not; but have renounced the hidden things of dishonesty, not walking in craftiness, nor handling the word of God deceitfully; but by manifestation of the truth commending ourselves to every man's conscience in the sight of God."

2 Corinthians 4:1-2 KJV

Dear Lord, you have called on me to be strong and not be afraid to work on your behalf. I will be careful to set a good example. Help me to speak the truth, and be fair in dealing with people. Don't allow me to try to outsmart someone. Let me be just in business transactions. If I am not treated in a fair way, let me walk away with dignity. It is not my job to judge others, but to try to conduct myself in a Christian manor. I thank you and praise you Lord for helping me. Amen.

Fear Not

November 26

Paul writes a letter to the church in Corinth after his visit there.

"We are experiencing all kinds of trouble, but we aren't crushed. We are confused, but we aren't depressed. We are harassed, but we aren't abandoned. We are knocked down, but we aren't knocked out."

2 Corinthians 4:8-9 CEB

Dear Lord, I praise you and thank you for the offer of eternal life. I know my body is temporary but my soul is eternal. No matter what my body experiences, my spirit will prevail. My body can be broken, and often by your grace it is healed. My physical being is comforted. But no matter what happens, no human on this earth can take away my salvation. I give my life to you, Lord. I know it is in the best hands. Continue to grant me your eternal, divine protection. I am yours. Amen.

Fear Not

November 27

Paul writes a letter to the church in Corinth after his visit there.

"For which cause we faint not; but though our outward man perish, yet the inward man is renewed day by day."

2 Corinthians 4:16 KJV

Dear Lord, I praise you and thank you today for having allowed me to live long enough to reach the age where my body is showing signs of wear. I refuse to complain about aches and pains. Eventually this body will cease to exist. During the process of aging, I may experience a decline in physical strength. I may experience heart disease or cancer. What if I cannot walk on my own or live independently. I used to fear these things. But I have come to understand that my inner strength can be renewed and made stronger every day that I live. I will not be afraid. Amen.

Fear Not

November 28

Paul, in his letter to the church at Corinth, discusses our heavenly dwelling.

"So we are always of good courage."

2 Corinthians 5:6

Dear Lord, today I praise you. I am taking quiet time at home to reflect on your glory. I will try to live through my spiritual self, more than my earthly self. I will thank you, God, continually for my faith which makes me feel safe. You, Lord, are my strength. You are my courage. You are my peace. Amen.

Fear Not

November 29

Paul's letter to the church at Corinth discusses our heavenly dwelling.

"Yes, we are of good courage, and we would rather be away from the body and at home with the Lord."

2 Corinthians 5:8

Dear Lord, let me always try to please you. Let me stay in your realm rather than spend time focusing on my earthly body. My soul and spirit are with you so I am safe. My body will eventually disappear, but you, God, are eternal. My home is in the eternal world with you. So I walk on this earth, constantly praising you. I keep my faith strong and I pray great courage will follow me. Amen.

November 30

Paul writes of his joy in his letter to the church at Corinth.

"I am acting with great boldness toward you; I have great pride in you; I am filled with comfort. In all our affliction, I am overflowing with joy."

2 Corinthians 7:4

Dear Lord, I praise you for the words that Paul brings. I will try to be as bold as he is and learn as he did to be content in all circumstances. I know that you want your children to be full of joy. I want my children to be happy. Why wouldn't you want the same for your children? I would love to be spared from all afflictions, trials and tribulations, but then my faith would probably never have a chance to grow and be strengthened. When I pray, I will always try to remember to ask that your will be done. Amen.

Fear Not

December 1

Paul tells of his joy in his letter to the church at Corinth.

"Even after we arrived in Macedonia, we couldn't rest physically. We were surrounded by problems. There was external conflict, and there were internal fears. However, God comforts people who are discouraged, and he comforted us by Titus' arrival."

2 Corinthians 7:5-6 CEB

Dear Lord, again Paul sets a great example for me to try to follow. Despite real problems, conflicts and possible danger, Paul manages to feel comforted. He does experience fear as any human does, but he allows you, Lord, to comfort him. When I experience those times of weakness, let me remember Paul and how he sought your comfort. You are always there with an extended hand, and arms to provide comfort. I thank you and praise you. Amen.

Fear Not

December 2

Paul continues in his letter to the church at Corinth. He is defending his ministry.

"I do not want it to appear that I am trying to frighten you with my letters. Someone will say, 'Paul's letters are severe and strong, but when he is with us in person, he is weak, and his words are nothing!'"

2 Corinthians 10:9-10 GNT

Dear Lord, I praise you and thank you. The words of your saints are bold and direct. I know I am weak. I have faults. I sin. Today's modern world tempts me with materialism. I am lured by the continual ungodly images in the media. If strong words in the gospel try to remind me to get Satan out of my life, let me pay attention. Please help me be vigilant. Let your grace keep me safe. I thank you for your gentle reminders for me to stay on your path. I will try to keep my focus on you and not on this world. Amen.

December 3

Paul wrote this letter while in prison to churches in and around Ephesus.

"This was according to the eternal purpose that he has realized in Christ Jesus our Lord, in whom we have boldness and access with confidence through our faith in him."

Ephesians 3:11-12

Dear Lord, my faith in you gives me confidence. It gives me boldness. I fear not. Despite the terrors of this world, I have the comfort of my Lord, Jesus Christ. Of this I am thankful. I am thankful for the life I am leading. I am thankful for every day that I find joy on this earth, before I go to rest in total and complete joy. I praise you, Lord. Amen.

Fear Not

December 4

Paul wrote this letter while in prison to churches in and around Ephesus.

"Wherefore I desire that ye faint not at my tribulations for you, which is your glory."

Ephesians 3:13 KJV

Dear Lord, I will try to be strong. Because of how much I worship you, I will do my very best and trust you in all things. Whether circumstances are good or horrible, I will try to keep a cheerful attitude. I will focus on how great you are and all the things for which I have to be thankful. No matter what happens, I will continue to praise your name. Help me to maintain this spirit of joy and gratuity. I can only do it with your help, Lord. Amen.

December 5

In this letter to churches in and around Ephesus Paul offers a prayer for spiritual strength.

"For this reason I bow my knees before the Father, from whom every family in heaven and on earth is named, that according to the riches of his glory he may grant you to be strengthened with power through his Spirit in your inner being, so that Christ may dwell in your hearts through faith-that you, being rooted and grounded in love, may have strength to comprehend with all the saints what is the breadth and length and height and depth, and to know the love of Christ that surpasses knowledge, that you may be filled with all the fullness of God."

Ephesians 3:14-19

Dear Lord, Paul's prayer says it better than I could. Please give me the strength I need to boldly proclaim your power. Amen.

Fear Not

December 6

While in prison, Paul writes to the churches in and around Ephesus about putting on the full armor of God.

"Finally, be strong in the Lord and in the strength of his might. Put on the whole armor of God, that you may be able to stand against the schemes of the devil. For we do not wrestle against flesh and blood, but against the rulers, against the authorities, against the cosmic powers over this present darkness, against the spiritual forces of evil in the heavenly places. Therefore take up the whole armor of God, that you may be able to withstand in the evil day, and having done all, to stand firm. Stand therefore, having fastened on the belt of truth, and having put on the breastplate of righteousness, and, as shoes for your feet, having put on the readiness given by the gospel of peace."

Ephesians 6:10-15

Dear Lord, again I just want to repeat the prayer of Paul. Amen.

Fear Not

December 7

While Paul is in prison he writes to the churches in and around Ephesus about the power of the gospel.

"Pray also for me, that whenever I speak, words may be given me so that I will fearlessly make known the mystery of the gospel, for which I am an ambassador in chains. Pray that I may declare it fearlessly, as I should."

Ephesians 6:19-20 NIV

Dear Lord, I pray that you will release me from any sins, demons or obsessions of this world that might have me bound in chains. Set me free from all restrictions that might prevent me from being the most courageous person possible. Please help me to accomplish all you want me to do for your kingdom. Please allow me the freedom to be joyful in your service. Amen.

December 8

Paul sent this message in a letter to the Philippi while he was in prison.

"And most of the brothers, having become confident in the Lord by my imprisonment, are much more bold to speak the word without fear."

Philippians 1:14

Dear Lord, you have a way of using any bad situation for your glory. I have learned that good can come out of most any events. I am not in physical chains like Paul, but let my existence help give confidence to others so together we can boldly spread your word. Let me trust in you Lord. My faith in you is what gives me courage. I praise you and thank you for your way of turning darkness into light. Amen.

Fear Not

December 9

Paul sent this message in a letter to the Philippi while he was in prison.

"What then? Only that in every way, whether in pretense or in truth, Christ is proclaimed, and in that I rejoice. Yes, and I will rejoice, for I know that through your prayers and the help of the Spirit of Jesus Christ this will turn out for my deliverance, as it is my eager expectation and hope that I will not be at all ashamed, but that with full courage now as always Christ will be honored in my body, whether by life or by death."

Philippians 1:18-20

Dear Lord, what a comfort to know that you will be with me in life and in death. You have a glorious home for me in heaven where there will be only love and there will be no fear. Anxiety will not exist. I will be at perfect peace. Help me to boldly enjoy every day on earth as I proclaim the glory of Jesus Christ. Amen

December 10

Paul sent this message in a letter to the Philippi while he was in prison.

"Let your reasonableness be known to everyone. The Lord is at hand; do not be anxious about anything, but in everything by prayer and supplication with thanksgiving let your requests be made known to God. And the peace of God, which surpasses all understanding, will guard your hearts and your minds in Christ Jesus."

Philippians 4:5-7

Dear Lord, these words of Paul tell the whole story of this devotional book I have been presenting. Don't worry. Pray. And give thanks. Lord I try to thank you several times a day for everything in my life. I know what brings me peace. My prayers to you, brought with thanksgiving never fail to bring peace and comfort. I praise you Lord. You are the essence of my life. Amen.

December 11

Paul sent this message in a letter to the Philippi while he was in prison.

"For I can do everything through Christ, who gives me strength."

Philippians 4:13 NLT

Dear Lord, how many times have I repeated that verse? Sometimes I change it to "I can do most things through Christ who gives me strength." That is because I do not always have enough faith and I am stuck in the mortal world. Some things would take a miracle for me to do. I don't think I could play professional football. That might not be reasonable, but it exists in this world. Some things are beyond human understanding and only exist in your universe, God. But here on earth I do believe that Christ will give me all the strength I need to do his will. Lord, you probably do not want me to play professional football. I trust you, Lord. Amen

December 12

Paul wrote his third letter to the faithful in Colossae to beware of false teachings.

"We're praying this so that you can live lives that are worthy of the Lord and pleasing to him in every way: by producing fruit in every good work and growing in the knowledge of God; by being strengthened through his glorious might so that you endure everything and have patience; and by giving thanks with joy to the Father. He made it so you could take part in the inheritance, in light granted to God's holy people."

Colossians 1:10-12 CEB

Dear Lord, I praise you. I am asking you to help me to pray continually that I will gain knowledge of your will for my life. I crave the wisdom and understanding that the Holy Spirit gives. I want to live a life that is pleasing to you. I thank you for the light, the strength and the courage that you bring. Amen.

Fear Not

December 13

Paul wrote this letter from Corinth to the Thessalonians to encourage them.

"But though we had already suffered and been shamefully treated at Philippi, as you know, we had boldness in our God to declare to you the gospel of God in the midst of much conflict."

1 Thessalonians 2:2

Dear Lord, I praise you and give thanks for all things. Today I know that any courage I have comes from you. I can stand up for my beliefs and be brave and strong, because you are with me. In this world that I am living in now, I need your strength. There is so much evil and violence. With the help of constant prayer, you make me feel secure. I am safe when you walk beside me. In Jesus' name I offer this prayer. Amen.

Fear Not

Paul wrote his second letter from Corinth to the Thessalonians.

"Don't be so easily shaken or alarmed by those who say that the day of the Lord has already begun. Don't believe them, even if they claim to have had a spiritual vision, a revelation, or a letter supposedly from us."

2 Thessalonians 2:2 NLT

Dear Lord, I praise you for your wisdom. I will try to also be wise in my own human way and not listen to doomsayers. Lots of movies, books and television shows predict the end of times or what will happen in the last days. I know that only you know the day and the hour. Scripture tells me that. I will not live in fear of anything that might happen in the future. I want you to give me the courage to live each day on earth with joy and love for you and my fellow man. I thank you for what little understanding you have given me. I humbly ask that you continue to bless me with the ability to live today in peace. Amen.

December 15

Paul writes this letter to Timothy, in Ephesus, about deacons in the church.

"Those helpers who do their work well win for themselves a good standing and are able to speak boldly about their faith in Christ Jesus."

1 Timothy 3:13 GNT

Dear Lord, I praise you and thank you for accepting me as a member of your family, even though my faith is not always perfect. I am not always as selfless and humble as I would like to be, but I do try to serve you and your children. I heard a missionary speaking a few days ago, and he said that even if you are not called by God to do anything in the mission field, do it anyway, because it is what you tell us to do. I will try to speak boldly and be a good helper even when I'm not sure of myself. You will give me strength. Amen.

Fear Not

December 16

While Paul was imprisoned in Rome, he wrote this letter to Timothy.

"For this reason I remind you to fan into flame the gift of God, which is in you through the laying on of my hands, for God gave us a spirit not of fear but of power and love and self-control."

2 Timothy 1:6-7

Dear Lord, I praise you and I thank you. Pease help me to study your words and grow in my faith. I pray that I may have what you commanded; a spirit of power, love and self-control. You give me my strength. Let me keep you at the center of my life. If the world around me is crazy, you will keep me sane. I devote myself to you. Amen.

December 17

Paul wrote this letter to Timothy while being held in prison in Rome.

"But the Lord stood by me and strengthened me, so that through me the message might be fully proclaimed and all the Gentiles might hear it. So I was rescued from the lion's mouth."

2 Timothy 4:17

Dear Lord, I have never been inside a lion's mouth. My needs to be rescued are far less dramatic. I only want strength to live out the rest of my life with dignity and to be in your good graces. I want to please you. I want to have you on my side, on my team, in all I do. I would love to think that maybe along the way your message, told through me, will touch someone. I would like to be used by you to help people feel safer and more secure in your love. Amen.

December 18

Paul writes this letter to Philemon, a leader in the church in Colossae. Paul is asking that Onesimus, a runaway slave of Philemon's, be accepted as a brother in Christ and not a slave when he returns to Colossae. Onesimus stole money from Philemon. Paul met Onesimus in prison, and he is now a Christian.

"Christ gives me the courage to tell you what to do."

Philemon 8 CEV

Dear Lord, I thank you and praise you for your forgiveness. When a person becomes new in Christ, all can be forgiven. I am grateful that my past regrets probably trouble me more than they trouble you. Sometimes I feel inadequate to ever give advice or ask anyone close to me to make any changes. If it is for something that needs to be done for you Lord, you will give me the courage to ask. Amen.

Fear Not

December 19

This letter to the Jewish Christians instructs that Jesus is the high priest.

"So whenever we are in need, we should come bravely before the throne of our merciful God. There we will be treated with undeserved kindness, and we will find help."

Hebrews 4:16 CEV

Dear Lord, if I have a need I know I can come to you. I must be brave in bringing you my requests, knowing that I will find help at your throne. I might not always get exactly what I am seeking, but I know you will always listen and be just. That is enough for me. I know you will be with me and provide me with what I need. It is important to me to have the faith that you will always be there with your own special brand of comfort. I see your comfort as an undeserved kindness. I gain my courage when I trust that your comfort is always there for the asking. Amen.

Fear Not

This letter to the Jewish Christians talks about living by faith.

"By faith Moses, when he was born, was hidden for three months by his parents, because they saw that the child was beautiful, and they were not afraid of the king's edict."

Hebrews 11:23

Dear Lord, sometimes I need to remember that you are the Lord and I must have faith. Today I had an ugly experience involving my doctor, my health insurance and the government's involvement. This was important to me because it affected my health and the health of my family. I was angry and upset. I couldn't see any way for things to improve. Then I remembered to give it to you, God, and have faith. Now I have peace. I am not afraid about my health or the state of healthcare in this country today. It is in your hands. No problem is too great for you. I praise you and thank you for reminding me to have faith. Amen.

Fear Not

December 21

This letter to the Jewish Christians talks about living by faith.

"By faith he left Egypt, not being afraid of the anger of the king, for he endured as seeing him who is invisible."

Hebrews 11:27

Dear Lord, by believing in you and seeing you even though you are invisible, I can have true faith. That faith gives me true courage. To me, true courage is going ahead, despite concerns, because I know you, Lord, are in control. With you by my side no one can hurt me because I have an eternal soul. My body could possibly be in danger at times, but death can only bring me closer to you and your holy throne in your holy kingdom. So what is there for me to fear? Amen.

December 22

This letter is to the Jewish Christians who are being persecuted.

"So we can confidently say, 'The Lord is my helper; I will not fear; what can man do to me?'"

Hebrews 13:6

Dear Lord, you are great. You promise never to leave me, never to forsake me. Not only are you my helper, at all times, forever, but I do not even need to call on you for help, because you are already there. I thank you for staying by my side. I thank you for your son Jesus. I thank you for my strength and courage. Let me keep the faith. Amen.

December 23

Peter is writing to the Christians in Asia Minor.

"For this is how the holy women who hoped in God used to adorn themselves, by submitting to their own husbands, Sarah obeyed Abraham, calling him lord. And you are her children, if you do good and do not fear anything that is frightening."

1 Peter 3:5-6

Dear Lord, I love you. I praise you. I do my best to obey you. I thank you for your word. Through your servant Peter, you have asked me not to fear anything. If I obey, I will be a child of Sarah. This could give me the comfort of a child in her mother's arms. In today's uncertain, isolated world, this is a comforting image. Let me try to do well and be brave. Lord, you give me courage. Amen.

December 24

Peter is writing this letter to the Christians in Asia Minor.

"Now who is there to harm you if you are zealous for what is good? But even if you should suffer for righteousness' sake, you will be blessed. Have no fear of them, nor be troubled, but in your hearts honor Christ the Lord as holy, always being prepared to make a defense to anyone who asks you for a reason for the hope that is in you; yet do it with gentleness and respect, having a good conscience, so that, when you are slandered, those who revile your good behavior in Christ may be put to shame."

1 Peter 3:13-16

Dear Lord, please help me to be pleasing to you. Jesus is pure. You are perfect. I walk in this world that is full of both good and evil. Help me walk on the good path. I praise you and thank you for my life and my faith. Amen.

Fear Not

December 25

Peter is writing this letter to the Christians in Asia Minor.

"Be humble in the presence of God's mighty power, and he will honor you when the time comes. God cares for you, so turn all your worries over to him."

1 Peter 5:6-7 CEV

Dear Lord, today is the birth of your Son, Jesus. Jesus, you are our Savior. You can carry all my problems, worries and fears. Today I am celebrating your birth. I am grateful that you came to earth and shared your great wisdom by your teachings. Gifts are nice, but You, Jesus are the real gift. I praise the Father, the Son and the Holy Spirit on this special day. Also Lord, I thank you for all my wonderful family. Amen.

Fear Not

December 26

Peter is writing this letter to the Christians in Asia Minor.

"Be on your guard and stay awake. Your enemy, the devil, is like a roaring lion, sneaking around to find someone to attack. But you must resist the devil and stay strong in your faith. You know that all over the world the Lord's followers are suffering just as you are. But God shows undeserved kindness to everyone. That's why he appointed Christ Jesus to choose you to share in his eternal glory. You will suffer for a while, but God will make you complete, steady, strong, and firm."

1 Peter 5:8-10 CEV

Dear Lord, once again I want to thank you for the strength you have given me. When I feel strong, I am much more courageous. The darkness in this world is the enemy that I struggle with. Please keep giving me the courage to stand up to evil. Help me to focus on what is good, pure and just. I am glad I was chosen to share in Christ's eternal glory. I praise you. Amen.

Fear Not

December 27

John, the disciple, wrote this letter to warn early Christians about false teachers trying to mislead them.

"And as we live in God, our love grows more perfect. So we will not be afraid on the day of judgment, but we can face him with confidence because we live like Jesus here in this world."

1 John 4:17 NLT

Dear Lord, I thank you and praise you for the very sacred words I read today. I wish I would have read and understood these verses earlier in my life, but I know there is no going back. You have a plan for me. I still have trouble telling what is your word compared to words of human teachers. I know to make sure everything I do is based on love, but love is not always enough. I need obedience. I need a balance. I need the proper kind of love. Lord, please make things clear to me when I need your understanding. Amen.

December 28

John, the disciple, wrote this letter to warn early Christians about false teachers trying to mislead them.

"There is no fear in love, but perfect love casts out fear. For fear has to do with punishment, and whoever fears has not been perfected in love."

1 John 4:18

Dear Lord, I love you. I love my brother. Please help me to love my enemies. Let me love like a child. I know you love me because you are love. With your love there is no fear. I am grateful for that. Let me walk in your light. Thank you, Lord, for your love. Amen.

December 29

John is writing to the Seven Churches of Asia. He sees an angelic figure in white.

"When I saw him, I fell at his feet as though dead. But he laid his right hand on me, saying, 'Fear not, I am the first and the last, and the living one.'"

Revelations 1:17-18

Dear Lord, your revelations are great. Your words are inspiring. I thank you for the Bible from beginning to end. Your words offer courage and strength. Angels surround me in times of trouble. Jesus will appear by my side when I need him most. In this I have faith. Amen.

December 30

John is writing to the Seven Churches of Asia. The Lord is speaking to John, telling him what to say to the angel.

"Do not fear what you are about to suffer. Behold, the devil is about to throw some of you into prison, that you may be tested, and for ten days you will have tribulation. Be faithful unto death, and I will give you the crown of life."

Revelation 2:10

Dear Lord, you are great. I thank you for everything and praise you with all my heart. I know there will be hard times in my life. With you I will endure. This journey of studying your word has not only given me courage, but has increased my faith. I now believe that even death cannot harm me. I am safe in your arms. I am so glad that I have your everlasting love. Amen.

Fear Not

December 31

John has visions of a heavenly throne, a majestic lamb, and tens of thousands of angels singing.

"In a loud voice they were saying: 'Worthy is the Lamb, who was slain, to receive power and wealth and wisdom and strength and honor and glory and praise!'"

Revelations 5:12 NIV

Dear Lord, my journey to end fear and find peace in three hundred and sixty five days has ended. I now can say, "Afraid of what? To enter heaven's rest." So the worst fear of dying is no longer a fear. The worry is erased. I feel stronger and more secure in my faith. As always, I am grateful to you, Lord. I hope my book will bless others. I will start the New Year with a spirit of courage, strength, power and humility. I wrote this book with you and for you. Amen.

Author Bio

I hope you like my devotional. I wanted to be a writer when I was growing up, but my life took different turns. My name is Sandra Darlene Davis. I am 70 years old at the time of this writing.

It took me a while to write my first book. For the past twenty years, I have lived in rural Alabama. Around here we say, "It's the back side of nowhere." On my mini farm, I have three miniature horses and a miniature Chihuahua. As a semi-retired person, I find time to play tennis and pickle ball. Occasionally, I get to go horseback riding, which is also one of my favorite activities. I like to kayak, hike and walk my dog.

I have two daughters and grandchildren. Both daughters are married and live in distant states. I love to travel, but most of my recent travels have been to visit my family.

Aside from now being a writer, I do still work some. I love working for the Great Physicians Clinic, which is a mission of Albertville First Baptist Church in Albertville, Alabama. We offer free vision care, glasses, and dental care for those unable to afford those services. I help the dentists and optometrists in the care of the patients. I am a

Licensed Practical Nurse, and I do health screenings and give influenza vaccines on a part-time, as needed basis.

That's a summary of what I'm up to these days. I have had a long busy life, so it would fill volumes to tell you of my past experiences. If you would like to know more about me, you can visit my webpage at www.whosoeverpress.com or visit www.sandradarlenedavis.com. I would love to get feedback from my readers. I know this journal has helped me grow as a Christian. I hope it does the same to you.